UNDERSTANDING THE MISUNDERSTANDING

D. C. Zook

SHANTIWALA
BOOKS

Berkeley, CA

Aside from brief quotations for media coverage and reviews, no part of this book may be reproduced or distributed in any form without the author's permission.

Text copyright © 2018 by D. C. Zook
All rights reserved.
Published by Shantiwala Books (Berkeley, CA)
Cover design by James, GoOnWrite.com
ISBN: 1947609084
ISBN-13 (print): 9781947609082
ISBN-13 (E.book): 9781947609006

Ourselves Among Others:
The Extravagant Failure of Diversity in America
And an Epic Plan to Make It Work

Understanding the Misunderstanding (vol. 1)

Liberating the Enclave (Vol. 2)

Writing the Past Imperfect (vol. 3)

Unpoisoning the Well (vol. 4)

*To the spirit and memory of Joe Strummer —
With this, I hope I've built a better brick*

TABLE OF CONTENTS

Series Preface	Ourselves Among Others	ix
Preface to Part 1	Understanding the Misunderstanding	xiii
Defining Diversity	A Prefatory Note	xvii
Chapter 1	Orchestrating Diversity	1
Chapter 2	Diversity and Discontent— A Preview	21
Chapter 3	America: The Improbable Country	68
Chapter 4	Putting Culture in its Place	136
Index		195
About the Author		197

SERIES PREFACE

OURSELVES AMONG OTHERS

This four-part series on the state of diversity in America has one specific goal: to create a much-needed revolution in the way we think about identity, and the way we situate ourselves among others. I wanted to write about identity in America using language that was accessible and engaging, while using concepts that were easy to grasp but profound in their consequences. In spite of the rosy and sanguine language of many a brochure or website from this university or that company on how much diversity they have and how much they value diversity, the reality is that diversity, in terms of what its professed goals are, has so far been an extravagant failure in America. Moreover, our ability to talk with each other about the problems of diversity has become more and more restricted, creating fear and frustration where there should be dialog and understanding. The result is that diversity has pulled American society further and further apart, sowing division where it should be creating unity. One nation indivisible has become one nation deeply divided. This series shows how and why that happened, and also offers a complete and ambitiously epic revision of diversity that will get things back on a more constructive track and create a diversity that works for and includes all of us.

Part 1 lays the groundwork by presenting the central premise of the entire series. It offers an overview of why diversity has gone so extravagantly wrong in America, and also shows why getting diversity right in America is something that stands potentially to create a template for other diverse societies struggling with issues similar to our own. In essence, Part 1 builds the foundation for everything to come.

Part 2 explains how diversity policy and practice over the past two or three decades has created an enclave society. By encouraging us to find our identity group and to approach diversity as a group-based project, diversity has built walls that separate us and encouraged the formation of identity-based enclaves. There is little interaction or understanding between these enclaves, and yet we celebrate the coexistence of separate enclaves as an achievement of diversity. As Part 2 shows, however, through a close examination of several of these different enclaves, an enclave society is not a diverse society. It is a divided society—the opposite of diversity. Enclaves are thus by-products of the failure of diversity.

Part 3 goes straight to the source of the problem, an unlikely culprit named History. Identity is in many ways a narrative we tell to ourselves and tell to others, but in the manic rush to create narratives that bolster our claims to diversity, we create falsified and distorted histories. If history is the foundation of identity, and if identity is the foundation of diversity, it is imperative that we tell equally critical histories for each and every identity that composes American society. Self-serving histories that paint perfect, unblemished portraits of a group are a shaky foundation for diversity, and the tendency for groups to deflect or reject critical questions from "outsiders" creates a form of censorship that makes meaningful dialog all but impossible. Without meaningful dialog, there can be no meaningful diversity.

Part 4 brings everything back together and develops an epic plan to put diversity on a new, constructive path to create meaningful understanding and substantive justice for all of us. By moving past the acrimonious debates over historical injustices, and by moving beyond the endlessly divisive inter-group rivalries to claim a greater share of the diversity pie, we can re-evaluate the place and role of diversity in American society. None of it will be easy, but absolutely all of it will be necessary. Without a new vision for diversity in America, the end result will be more division rather than less, and a diversity that divides us is not really diversity at all. It's nothing less than an extravagant disaster. This series shows not only how to avert the disaster, but also how to make diversity work for us all.

PREFACE TO PART 1

UNDERSTANDING THE MISUNDERSTANDING

In March 2017, an unlikely picture of two people riding the New York subway emerged on social media that quickly went viral.[1] The image, which showed a Muslim woman wearing a hijab with a full-face veil sitting next to a drag queen with bright red lipstick and even brighter red hair, was widely praised as a shining example of diversity and tolerance. Here were two people from totally different walks of life, sitting next to each other on the subway, and neither was making an issue of it. The drag queen was looking at her phone, and the Muslim woman was looking askance with that blank stare subway riders often have when they want to appear lost in thought but have no thoughts to be lost in. Because they both appeared to be completely indifferent to one another, the assumption was that each tolerated the other without judgment, and thus, diversity triumphed and all was right in the world.

As this book will show in painstaking detail, what that picture actually showed was not the presence of diversity in America but

---

1 See for instance, John Bonazzo, "Conservative Gets Dragged by Twitter Over Photo of Drag Queen, Muslim on Subway," *Observer* (March 12, 2017) at http://observer.com/2017/03/twitter-subway-photo-conservatives-liberals/

rather its absence. Diversity isn't a picture, a static representation of people who are different. Rather, diversity is a process. More specifically, it's an *intercultural process* of shared understanding. Nothing in that picture of the two people on the New York subway shows that there is any sort of interaction or understanding between them. Two people from separate worlds whose worlds will always remain separate unless one or both of them initiates contact or crosses the bridge between them. As long as their worlds remain separate, as long as they live in their separate enclaves of existence, we cannot speak of diversity. Something more, much more, is required, and that is the starting point of this book.

Conservatives looked at that picture with a sense of foreboding and lamentation. For them, it was a future to be feared, the end of America as it was and always should be. Liberals looked at the picture with a sense of accomplishment and celebration. For them, it was a representation of diversity, a picture of America as it is now and will be in the future. As this book will show, however, both sides are wrong, and woefully so.

Chapter 1 explains in detail the central argument of this whole series and also the foundational elements and understandings we need to create a new diversity that is dynamic and interactive. We need to move far beyond thinking that a picture of different people sitting side by side on the subway is diversity.

Chapter 2 goes into considerable detail about a transformative and influential Supreme Court case regarding affirmative action, one that shifted the focus of diversity away from historical remedy and toward present-day social integration. Central to the Supreme Court's argument was the idea that diversity's main purpose is to provide a forum for the "robust exchange of ideas" between different identity groups (something clearly missing in the photograph from the New York subway). That "robust exchange of ideas" remains conspicuously absent from diversity as we currently have it in America, and indeed, the possibility for any meaningful dialogue across lines of difference has become more and more remote with each passing day.

Chapter 3 offers a drone's eye view of the social landscape of America, as filtered through ideas about and experiences of diversity. America is unique in the depth and richness of difference in American society, which in many ways makes America the ultimate test case of whether and how complex, pluralistic societies can thrive and prosper as an integrated whole. There is a comparative perspective here, too, that shows how those who remain convinced that America is the most racist country in the world believe so based on imperfect and incomplete information about non-American experiences with diversity.

Chapter 4 is a sobering discussion of the role of culture in the construction of diversity. When it comes to culture, many people mistake familiarity for superiority, and grotesquely overestimate the extent to which culture determines our individual destinies. The rise of cultural fundamentalism and the growing opposition to anything that smacks of cultural appropriation are both by-products of the failure to move beyond simplistic pictures of different people passively coexisting in the same space as some sort of iconic image of diversity.

The most important endeavor throughout this volume is to reopen questions and conversations that were lamentably closed long ago. A closed mind is the perennial nemesis of diversity, so if you find yourself rejecting things that sound unfamiliar as you read through this book, or if you find yourself rejecting out of hand what doesn't conform to your pre-conceived notions of diversity and social justice, then perhaps it's time to spend a little more time examining yourself rather than blaming others for the extravagant failure of diversity in America. We've all got work to do, and there's no better time than now to get started.

DEFINING DIVERSITY

A PREFATORY NOTE

One of the more surprising things about diversity is that even though it is arguably the most important topic in American thought and American social life, there is no standard definition of what diversity is. This is as true for educational policy as it is for government legislation and judicial rulings. We all talk about diversity, even though we don't know exactly what it is. Odd, that. For this book, at least, here is a starting point toward a meaningful definition of diversity, one that works for all the discussions I will offer throughout this book, and one that hopefully will generate a more focused public debate about diversity.

Diversity: The collective array in any society of identity-based characteristics—including innate characteristics such as race, ethnicity, gender, and sexual orientation, as well as well as non-innate characteristics such as age, religion, political viewpoint, profession, and personal interests—and the processes through which these different characteristics interact with and influence one another.

Informally, and more simply, diversity is a collective term for the different ways we situate ourselves among others.

CHAPTER 1

ORCHESTRATING DIVERSITY

Ah, what a mess. Diversity, that is. Before I launch into a preview of all the intertwined issues that make diversity such a misdirected drama, I'll start with a simple question: Is diversity a good idea done wrong, or a bad idea done just right? As I will make clear throughout this book, there is nothing inherently wrong with the idea of diversity, and in fact as an idea it evokes tremendous promise. The problem therefore must lie in the execution and in the application, and that indeed is pretty much the central message of this whole book. Sure, people groan with dyspeptic anguish any time someone brings up the topic of diversity—just watch faces contort with resigned pain when you inform a group of people they need to attend a "diversity training" workshop—but if you push a bit further down the line of that conversation, you will discover that most people have a problem with a particular experience and a particular policy or some other specific thing that has gone horribly wrong with diversity.[2] Indeed, I've never met a single

---

2 For an amusing depiction from popular culture, see this sketch from Saturday Night Live (Season 40, 2014): https://www.nbc.com/saturday-night-live/video/women-in-the-workplace/2823759?snl=1

person who has rejected the idea of diversity, or who has found it inherently offensive or ridiculous or unnatural or any other adjective in that vein of thinking. No one has a problem with diversity, but lots of people have lots of problems with the way that diversity is delivered and the shape it is in when it arrives. Beethoven's Ninth Symphony is an exquisite work, but if you hand the score over to a bunch of accordion-playing monkeys, I doubt the result will be pretty. And who could blame Beethoven for the monkey-accordion fiasco? Better to blame the monkeys, or more importantly, the miscreant who gave the accordions to the monkeys in the first place. As any musician worth her weight in bananas would know—monkeys prefer harpsichords.

In any case, here in concise form is the gist and the grist of what ails diversity, what makes it fail, and more importantly, what it will take to make it succeed. It's a beautiful idea, one worth keeping and one worth salvaging, so while there is a great deal of work to be done, it is good work and work that is worth doing. It's even more important to make it work and succeed in the United States. If it fails here, it will send a message to the rest of the world to stop trying. It would lend credence to the perverted ideologies of racism and ethnic cleansing, and it would put very fresh wind in the sails of those who feel that narcissistic homogeneity, a world of endless selves without any others to sully the fetid utopia of sameness and uniformity, is the true and proper object of our identity-based desires. In case you haven't been paying attention to a little thing called all of human history, every time someone moves in the direction of that utopia, the world, or at least part of it, ends up covered with dead bodies. There's a better way to do diversity, and even if I don't have all of the answers, I at least have tried to answer all of the questions.

On the surface, diversity seems a simple enough concept. Simply put more and more different kinds of people together and something special will eventually happen. But if diversity were as simple and straightforward as that, it would not be the subject of so much contentious litigation and it would not be one of the most divisive political issues of our time. For many reasons, all of which will form the discussion of the rest of this series of books, diversity has also become the one issue that no one can talk about openly, collectively, and mutually, something all the more lamentable since cross-cultural dialog is precisely one of the things that diversity is supposed to facilitate. Anyone who thinks they have an easy recipe for diversity is engaging in self-delusion. Adding more and more of the same unimaginative and simplistic ingredients we already have is not going to make the feast of diversity any more enticing or appealing. It is a bit like a failed soufflé: once it collapses, you can leave it in the oven all you want, but it is never going to turn into what you hoped, and the most likely outcome is that it will simply burn and go up in flames. The whole point of this book series is to bring a new set of conceptual ingredients to the diversity kitchen, so to speak, along with a new set of cooking methods and a new recipe book, to try to rescue the bountiful feast that diversity has promised, but so far has failed to deliver. Strange thing, diversity: with it, there can never be too many cooks in the kitchen—as long as they keep cooking.

The Main Event (aka, the main concept that drives this book):

> *Diversity is facing the wrong direction. It is upside-down and inside-out. For the readers who prefer a bit of crudeness with their knowledge, it's ass backwards. What that means in a nutshell is that all along we have been taught or we have come to believe that diversity is all about us—ourselves—and that, it turns out, is the fatal flaw in the architecture of diversity. Diversity*

> *is not a platform for us to present and perform and promote our own identities. No, it's a process through which we all endeavor to understand everyone and everything that we are not. For diversity to succeed, the core of the whole project has to be never ourselves and always others. How that works and what that looks like—well, that's what this book is all about.*

Of course, along the way there will be a few other themes that are presented and developed, but none of them stray too far from the central concept. No one ever said diversity would be simple and easy—if that were the case, we wouldn't need a book like this and we wouldn't have so many lawsuits and protests and Jerry Springeresque shouting matches every time diversity tries to find a pathway through society. Without further ado, here are the other themes will help develop and explain the concept outlined above in The Main Event.

1. Diversity is a social demeanor and a civic responsibility.
Too many people think that diversity is a nice word for who we already are. If we think there should be more of the kind of people we already are—in schools, offices, government institutions, and other public places—then we also tend to think that it is the government's responsibility to create policies and generate the necessary funds to make that happen. But diversity is more than just who we already are. It is also, and more importantly, the other things we can become. It is about how we act, what we do, who we know, what we know, and how we come to know it, all in the presence of those who are everything we are not and always with a hint of who we already are. It is about finding the best way to

position ourselves among others. The government *cannot* do that for us, and the government *should not* do that for us—at least not entirely. Diversity cannot and should not be constructed entirely out of government programs and policies; to do so keeps us forever dependent on the very officials on whom we can consistently least depend. Diversity requires independence of thought and movement, an independence that should be carefully guarded and thoughtfully crafted. Seriously, when did we become so naïve as to think that our public officials can engineer perfect policy and then execute it flawlessly? If you ask the government to give you an eighty-piece orchestra, odds are better than even that what you will actually receive is a shipment of eighty karaoke machines, complete with forty microphones which turn out to be incompatible with the karaoke machines and an instruction booklet for a lawn mower in sixteen different languages, none of which is English. Monkeys with accordions indeed.

The old adage that if you want something done right you need to do it yourself is especially true for diversity. In political terms, that means we bear much of the responsibility for ensuring that we get the type of diversity that works best for everyone. The moment we enter public space, we are an actor in the complex machinery of a diverse society. And yet for some reason diversity always ends up being someone else's responsibility or someone else's sacrifice to make. It's like someone standing in front of a door waiting for someone else to open it for them, never realizing that they could just open it themselves, and never thinking that they could hold it open for others as well. We need to open that door for ourselves and we need to keep it open for others, regardless of who we are as ourselves and who they are as others. On the best of days, there is at most indifference to being in or being out of the workings of diversity. But if America is to hold true to its promise and vision, diversity needs to be not only what we all do, but what we all do best. If you want the well-crafted orchestra of diversity to play sweet and beautiful music, then pick up an instrument, tune in, and start playing. Oh, and if you think you'll just stay home and skip the rehearsals and the recitals and then wait for the music to start streaming on Spotify, then you are just wasting everyone's time. And as this book will make very clear, there's precious little time to waste.

2. Racism in America is as diverse as America.
You cannot talk about diversity for any length of time before someone invokes the scourge and stigma of racism. Diversity, it is often claimed, is the antidote to or the payment for racism in America, and since racism is assumed to be the ugly book authored exclusively by the ever-dominant "majority," diversity is designed to provide non-dominant minority groups with the hitherto denied opportunity to rewrite that book, or to write a book of their own, that resists and erases racism and tells a better, less-biased, more-complete and more-satisfying narrative. In this perspective, if racism still exists in America, it is because the dominant group still controls access to the book, and the only way to fix it is to provide more and more programs to give more and more opportunities to the non-dominant groups so they can write what they want to write. The problem with the whole enterprise is that no one wants to admit that it was a bad book to begin with, based on a faulty and dubious premise, and no amount of writing or rewriting is going to salvage it.

Though no one wants to hear it, the painful truth is that racism persists in American society not because it is so deeply entrenched through the actions and words of the dominant group, but because it is so deeply entrenched in the actions and words of all groups. If we conceive of diversity as a process where members of the dominant group, who are assumed to be racist, are slowly pushed aside to make way for the non-dominant groups, who are assumed to be non-racist, then it is easy to believe that diversity is synonymous with anti-racism. By this account, anyone who opposes or even questions diversity is therefore a racist. And also by this account, if racism persists in American society, then the only remedy for it is more and more of the same diversity we've had for so many years, which so far has done precious little to tackle the problem of racism.

Racism does not persist in American society because there have not been enough diversity programs to make diversity "happen" and to make racism disappear. Racism persists because the whole account of why we have so much racism is itself entirely flawed. Racism persists not because the entrenched dominant group won't let go, but because diversity programs that focus on empowering non-dominant and putatively non-racist groups against the (assumedly racist) dominant group are actually only addressing one small part of the problem of racism. You cannot fix the whole problem of racism by focusing only on one part. Any approach to implementing diversity that ignores the pervasiveness of racism in all communities in the United States is destined for epic failure.

One often hears tenuously hypothetical questions raised in discussions of diversity that hint at the skewed and imperfect vision on which most ideas of diversity are based. One hears questions such as, "Is there such a thing as black racism?" or "Is there reverse racism?" One hears condescending answers explaining the "fallacy" of reverse racism. But these are the wrong questions to ask, and the wrong answers to give. The whole discussion borders on the absurd. Racism is as diverse as America; indeed, racism is as diverse as humanity. Depressing? Sure. But inventing different labels for racism—as if "white racism" could be completely different from "racism of color"—misses the point entirely: racism is racism, regardless of the practitioner, and it is always ugly and it is always awful. It has no direction and does not move either forward or reverse; it works the same way every time and it is always the wrong way. Inventing different strains of racism to determine whether dominant racism is somehow worse that non-dominant racism also misses the point. It is like comparing different genocides to see if one is worse than other. There is no such thing as a mild atrocity. If you want to end racism, it's the same as if you want to end genocide: you need to choose your opponents carefully, not conveniently.

3. Diversity is not a point we reach, but rather a practice we cultivate.
In the next chapter, I will discuss a case from the Supreme Court in which the court said that by 2028 we should be in a position, socially and politically, where we no longer need any advocacy programs or policies to help us achieve diversity. We won't need any more diversity programs to help us *get* diversity because we will already *have* diversity. The trouble with this conceptualization is not the time frame, which seems wonderfully optimistic. Nor is it the belief that diversity-related programs will no longer be necessary, which seems eminently celebratory. The problem is in the assumption that there is some point in time where we will be able to sit back and say wow, we did it, we acquired diversity—congratulations on a job well done. The sobering news is that *the work of diversity is never done.* Yes, the secret to diversity is the same as the secret to a good marriage. It will take hard work, and it will take constant work. There is a word we use to describe someone who thinks marriage will be easy, and that word is divorced. And there is a word we use to describe someone who thinks diversity will be easy, but that word is not something I would repeat in polite society.

The good news is that the image of a dreary future of chain-gang diversity work can also be seen as a labor of love (and no, that's not hippie-talk or Berkeley-speak). With a little practice and a slight change of perspective, cultivating diversity can be seen as a vocation, like the gardener in the garden, the mechanic in the garage, the musician in the studio, the tinkerer in the...

tinkerer-place. No one ever says—As of today I have learned the piano, or As of today I have learned Korean. One can always learn new techniques, and one can always learn new words, to become ever more mellifluous, with music as with language. Even Paul McCartney still has to practice—the better the musician, the more they know the value of practice—and as anyone who has tried to learn a foreign language knows, you've got to use it or you'll lose it. Diversity is no different. Perhaps we will never reach an absolute point where we *have* diversity, but at least we can always keep working to maintain fluency.

4. Diversity is not about being different; it is about understanding difference. There is a fundamental difference between what I will call *passive* diversity and *active* diversity. Passive diversity, which best characterizes what we currently have as diversity, is the practice of assuming that if you have an identity which is in any way different from the dominant group, or what is sometimes called "Wonder Bread" white society, then you contribute to diversity by mere existence. You do not have to do anything, you simply have to be present. "Being Latino," for instance, automatically counteracts or diversifies the overwhelming presence of "being White." The task of diversity is by this account simplified down to a set of policies that gets as many diverse (non-white) people into a room as possible. The problem with this approach, as I will show in painstaking detail in the rest of this book, is that no one has a plan for what is supposed to happen after everyone has entered the room. The work of diversity, as it is currently conceived and implemented, is simply to get people into the room, where they exist, differently. At that point, diversity can take a rest. Its work is done.

Active diversity, which we do not yet have but which we desperately need (and what this book will describe in detail), is the act of becoming what you are through the practice of understanding what you are not. The practice of learning requires effort, sometimes considerable effort, but it is the only way to reach the endpoint of understanding all those other people who are the things that we are not. Simply being different means precious little by this account, even if you are in the room with everyone else, because it accomplishes nothing. It is a *display* of difference, but not a meaningful and substantive *act of diversity*. Diversity requires us to step away from ourselves, and to step away from those like us, to walk into the world of the things we are not and do our best to understand and experience the world through the eyes of others around us. There are two important aspects about this process of active diversity to take note of: (1) the act of understanding is equally the responsibility of all members of society, whether from the majority or the minority; and (2) when you look at the world through the eyes of others, you do not necessarily have to like what you see. I can learn to understand why someone might like Nickleback's music, after working past my first assumption that they were hearing-impaired, but that does not mean I have to like it, too. (Just kidding, Nickelback, and kudos for taking all the mud thrown at you in stride.)

Our currently dominant mode of passive diversity has created a sense of complacency among far too many people. This is how we end up with the simplistic assumption that anyone from a non-dominant group automatically "adds diversity" to any situation or environment simply by being there. No work or effort is involved. The government and other institutions are expected to pass policy after policy and create program after program just to get more people from certain groups into the room. And once they are in the room, the sense of complacency sets in: *I have arrived, and that is enough*. But it is not enough. Diversity and complacency are like parallel lines: they are never supposed to meet, and if they do, something has gone horribly wrong. And indeed, something already has.

5. Diversity must be intercultural, not multicultural
Multiculturalism has been one of the most oversold ideas ever to hit the social marketplace. On the surface, it promises a wonderfully rich social milieu in which we all live together, celebrating the diversity we think we see all around us. But in reality, multiculturalism always disappoints because it has no soul, no anima—no process to set it in motion. It remains static, largely because multiculturalism is more display case than machine. We see different identity groups, we are encouraged to tolerate the difference we see, we are even asked to "celebrate" diversity, but we are never asked to participate in diversity and we are certainly never invited to question it.

Much of Europe has drifted to the political right in recent years, and the culprit at the top of the list for that rightward drift is multiculturalism, which for many Europeans now seems a failed experiment. The same can be said for America in the November 2016 elections, where a surge of populist-nationalist sentiment took aim at multiculturalism and the culture of political correctness that surrounds it. But where Europe and America both get things wrong is in thinking that a resurgent nationalism should push multicultural diversity aside and roll back the social clock to a time when supposedly the nation was simpler and more unified and where minorities knew their proper place. Rolling back the clock isn't possible or even desirable, and nationalism is not an antidote to multiculturalism. What is needed instead is a new, dynamic version of diversity, one that keeps us in motion and in circulation together and resists the formation of enclaves and the entropy of separation that multiculturalism produces. *Intercultural* diversity does exactly that. By rewarding individuals for their active interaction between identity groups rather than their passive membership within them, intercultural diversity works against the enclave mindset that multicultural diversity creates and fosters mutual understanding and cross-group integration. In a nutshell, how we make that happen is what this book is about.

Two images

Perhaps the easiest way to see the difference between what we currently have and what we actually need in the diversity department is to show the difference graphically. Keeping in mind that American society has been greatly simplified for the purposes of illustration (I am using six identity groups here, fully aware that American society has hundreds), I will illustrate and explain the key differences between the two approaches to diversity.

1. What we have: Multicultural (passive) diversity

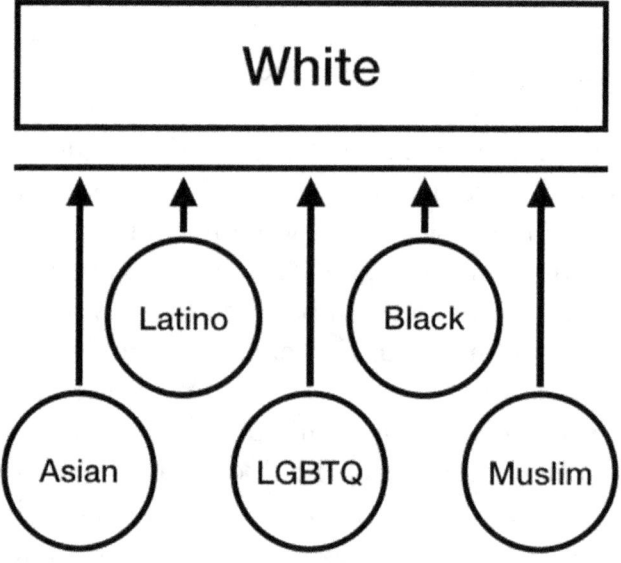

Multicultural (passive) diversity

Our current multicultural idea of diversity is competitive, combative, and conflictual. The white identity group is seen as dominant and inherently oppressive toward all other groups, and the goal of diversity is to break through the barrier separating white from non-white ("people of color") and displace white dominance.

Understanding the Misunderstanding

Replacing white dominance with people from non-white groups is seen as social justice by proponents of diversity, and the process is implemented as a numbers game: the more whites are displaced and replaced by non-whites, the more society becomes diverse and just.

Non-white groups compete separately and competitively in this process, each one working antagonistically against the others in seeking to displace white dominance (represented by the black arrows in the image) and promote more representation for members from their own groups. The benefits of diversity are thus distributed among identity-based groups, leading to suspicion and antagonism between non-white groups, and entrenching vilification of the dominant white group. This is how multicultural diversity ends up replicating the divisions and antagonisms that tear American society apart rather than resolving or replacing them.

Participation in multicultural diversity is purely passive. One participates merely by membership in a group. This leads inherently to a strengthening of boundaries around and between different groups, and the creation of the enclave mindset. Separation and difference between groups is seen as a form of empowerment, as it creates a clearer platform from which to demand more spaces for each separate group as more and more white spaces are displaced.

Enclaves are strengthened as each group fights its own, separate fight, and the antagonism between white and non-white grows ever deeper, creating more racial and identity-based division in American society rather than less. We are taught to tolerate our differences, but nothing in this structure creates any understanding or any emotional connection between groups. We retreat to our separate spaces and do our best to tolerate what we don't understand. Multicultural diversity, in other words, pulls us apart into separate spaces and leaves us there, co-existing alongside each other, but more divided than ever.

2. What we need: intercultural (active) diversity

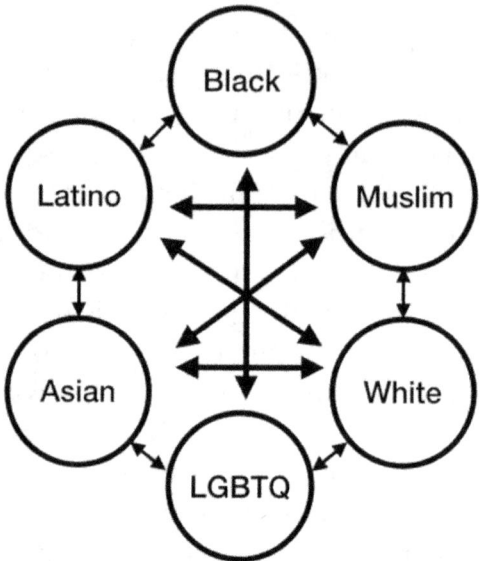

Intercultural (active) diversity

Intercultural (active) diversity, on the other hand, is cooperative, collaborative, and creative. The end goal is not displacement of the dominant white group, but rather diffusion of all groups into the shared spaces in-between. Since all groups have equal access to the intercultural space in between (the black arrows in the image), indeed they create that space together, words like dominance and non-dominance, or majority and minority, lose their meaning and become irrelevant.

Unlike multicultural diversity, which offers rewards for mere passive membership in a group, intercultural diversity rewards persons for their active contributions to diversity, measured by the energy and time spent cultivating interaction in the intercultural space. Active outreach and interaction, rather than passive membership and separation, are the desired goals of diversity. Whereas multicultural diversity creates separation and difference, intercultural diversity creates empathy and understanding. Enclaves are replaced by shared, intercultural spaces.

Making it personal
There is one final element to discuss, and that is the little matter of who I am and why I am writing *this* book in *this* way at *this* time. I suppose all acts of creativity happen in their own time, and for whatever reason, I reached a point where it finally made sense to write out the many things that had been there on my mind for many years. This of course raises the question of why those things were on my mind, and why I left them there for so many years, and so that will be as good a place as any to start.

For reasons I will never fully understand, I have been drawn all of my life toward issues of justice and fairness. That includes when I was very young, and it includes my professional life now. I have spent the better part of the past decade conducting research that relates to human rights and the politics of identity. I tend to focus geographically on Asia, pretty much anywhere from the southern tip of India all the way to the northern tip of Japan—including all places in between—and I have had the opportunity to spend a good amount of time studying how multicultural and multi-religious societies struggle to hold together and struggle to achieve the elusive sensation of fairness. All of them try, and many, if not most, fail. Even a country like Fiji, which really has only two major identity groups—indigenous Fijians and the Indo-Fijians—has gone through three military coups, all based on identity politics, and is still struggling to this day to find a way to get these two groups to co-exist peacefully. Every time I return to the United States, a country with a dazzling array of different groups, I am struck by how well, comparatively speaking, the whole system works. I am even struck by the fact that it works at all. I am also struck by how many people in America, lacking the experience I have had of seeing so many other places and so many other cultures, think that America is the worst place on earth. Trust me, it isn't. Not by a long shot.

I do not say that as an act of national pride. I do speak from the heart, but when I say that the United States is in many ways a one-of-a-kind place, I say it with the experience of someone who has been to many places and has never seen anything quite like America. But like any country, failure is always an option, and having seen just how ugly failure can be in other countries—tensions over identity can and often do lead to some of the most inhumane acts of violence imaginable—the scary fact is that sometimes it is little more than just enough grit and goodwill that keeps America from sliding down a similar path of sorrow. The United States has weathered some tough times, but it is not and never has been inherently immune from disaster. Complacency is never a good wellspring from which to craft a nation.

It is one thing to judge the acts of America in relation to what other countries have done (or have not done), and while the conclusion that as bad as it is in America sometimes it is still better than other countries is comforting, it is hardly a satisfying conclusion. It is far better, and far tougher, to judge America by its own ideas and by its own ideals. Granted, half of the struggle of diversity is to figure out what those ideas and ideals are, and to determine if they are the best they can be. Has America failed to live up to some of its ideals? Of course it has—what American has not felt disappointment and disenchantment at one point or other? But it is always better to raise the bar high when it comes to cultivating ideas and ideals, and one could plausibly claim that America cornered the market on those inspirational commodities long ago.

Understanding the Misunderstanding

If you aspire for the sun and only reach the moon, you have still done far more than those who sit on earth and try to convince themselves that there is no better place to be. Rationalization is the mantra of mediocrity.

This book is only academic to the extent that is written by someone whose professional credentials mark him as a member of the academic community. But in format, tone, and style, I have self-consciously chosen not to write what for lack of a better description might be called an "academic book." In a standard academic book, I would be required to spend much of my time engaging in lengthy discussions of other scholarly literature on the topic, almost all of it written by academics for other academics. That would be no easy task on a topic like this, since there are literally hundreds of books and thousands of articles on this topic, most of them written in the lamentably dense and obtuse style of writing preferred by those in the academic profession. But it is not the sheer volume of those writings that makes me want to write a different sort of book, but rather the more alarming fact that most of the scholarly literature written on diversity is dreadful and useless in equal measure. While in many other areas of academic study, researchers can and do aspire as much as possible to let their data and other information speak for itself, in much of the scholarship on diversity the opposite is true: researchers want to make the data they collect justify partisan conclusions they have already reached. The result is an entire library of predetermined outcomes, written with the lexicon of ideological cant.

In other words, diversity research is inherently and consistently an activist agenda from one side of the intellectual spectrum to the other masquerading as dispassionate or neutral research. Phrases such as "studies have shown" or "it has been shown conclusively" actually mean something more along the lines of "colleagues who already think like me have written." What you will not find are liberal scholars who engage in diversity research and find that—surprise!—diversity programs really *are* unfair entitlement programs for minorities. Nor will you find conservative scholars who engage in diversity research and find that—surprise!—diversity programs really *do* correct historical injustices or revolutionize the learning environment of the classroom. This is not by accident; it is by design.

And so, with all of this in mind, I offer something different, something that is more of a personal narrative of someone who has spent the better part of a professional career engaging with diversity and diversity-related issues in a wide variety of familiar and not-so-familiar places. Just as an auto mechanic with years of experience develops a feel for the complexities of how an engine works and knows intuitively how to discern the origin of any problem; just as a pipefitter with years of experience develops a feel for the complexities for how a high-pressure, industrial-grade piping system fits together and knows intuitively where to look when things go wrong; so, too, in my profession, I would like to think that with years of experience under my belt I have developed a feel for the complex architecture of public policy and can discern intuitively where things go wrong in the translation of policy into practice. This book is not intended as an ivory-tower concoction of some theoretical utopia of diversity. The focus throughout is on diversity as lived experience in everyday life. Everyday life may not be a utopia, but any day can always be made a better day. And if that is what we aspire to with our days of diversity, it might just be enough to make the whole thing work.

Neither left nor right

I wish I could write a feel-good book about diversity. I really do. It would certainly make my life a lot easier. It would be so very easy to write a liberal book about all the inherent goodness of diversity and how wonderful all cultures are, and I am sure there are many liberal people who would love to read it, all the while straining their necks as they nod in euphoric approval at every sentence. I can almost hear the soft-toned jazz-lounge voices of NPR commentators talking with restrained giddiness about yet another book written by yet another liberal scholar who just so happens to support everything NPR has already said.

It would also be so very easy to write a conservative book about how diversity is really just a subterfuge for unjustified and underserved entitlements that are then billed to the hard-working taxpayer, and there are many conservative people who would love to read that, too, all the while straining their wrists as they applaud quietly in self-congratulatory encomium. I can almost hear the open-vowel Sunday-school elocutions of Fox News commentators talking with well-postured passion about yet another book by yet another conservative scholar that just so happens to support everything Fox News has already said.

The irony is thick here. For some reason, when people seek out books on the topic of diversity, a concept that in its essence is supposed to expose us to different things, they repeatedly seek out books that tell them what they already think. How can anyone affirm the correctness of their point of view on diversity by immersing themselves in books steeped in sameness? That is why I cannot write the easy book; my conscience tells me that I must do something else entirely, namely to write a book that looks at diversity on its own terms and through its own actions. I have no claim to write with objectivity—I will tell things as I see them—but I would like to think that I at least have made the best effort possible to write a book with integrity.

I suppose all I could ask of anyone who would read this book is to read it with the same spirit of integrity with which I write it, to read it through cover to cover and to be prepared to let go of or reconsider even their most deeply cherished beliefs. Too much of the ongoing conversation in the field of diversity is centered on getting other people to admit they are wrong; we rarely hold ourselves to the same standard of scrutiny, and few of us engage in the more intricate task of challenging ourselves first, before we challenge others. Outrage is always welcome, for it is the powerhouse of spirited action. At the very least, outrage is preferable to cynicism, which is the dreary motive of inaction. I have no intention to be provocative just for the sensationalist sake of being provocative, for the topic on which I write is already such on its own.

CHAPTER 2

DIVERSITY AND DISCONTENT—A PREVIEW

> *The way to stop discrimination on the basis of race is to speak openly and candidly on the subject of race.* —Justice Sonia Sotomayor, US Supreme Court (Schuette v. Coalition to Defend Affirmative Action, 2014)

What's Wrong with Diversity?

To begin with, an observation: There *is* nothing inherently wrong with the idea of diversity, or with it, any related ideas such as multiculturalism, cultural pluralism, and so on. The idea of building and cultivating a vibrant, open, and integrated society that might otherwise be deeply and perhaps violently divided by its intrinsic differences is a goal worth pursuing and a project worth fighting for. Yet immediately we are confronted with difficult questions: Why then has it been so difficult to get people to work together to achieve this laudable goal? Why has it been such a bitter and vituperative experience for so many people, to the point where the mere mention of the word "diversity" is greeted with a roll of the eyes, a resigned sigh, or a cynical smirk? Why does talk of diversity transform an otherwise civil conversation into an acrimonious altercation? The trouble as I see it is not with diversity itself, but rather with all the emotional and cultural baggage that has been unfortunately piled up around it. And what is more, it is not just the amount of baggage, but also how it has been packed and how it has been arranged and how it has been delivered. What should have been a wonderful discussion about the many pathways to a shared destination has devolved instead into an endless disagreement about whose pathway is best or whose emotional and cultural baggage is most deserving of special treatment. It is a bit like getting halfway up Mt. Everest, realizing you need oxygen, and then opening your backpack to find that for some reason you have packed a tuxedo, a hack saw, and a complete dvd boxed-set edition of *Soul Train*. Each are interesting items that are perhaps worth having in their own right, and at some point, there was probably a legitimate thought process in which it might have made sense to put them all in the same bag. But that thought process seems frustratingly irrecoverable when you are standing on the slopes of Everest, and in that situation, when the one thing you need is oxygen, all of these items are uniformly quite useless.

To demonstrate just how quickly this baggage piles up, and how quickly it obfuscates even the simplest of points, I will start with a quote that I think precisely encapsulates the spirit of diversity:

> *Wer fremde Sprachen nicht kennt, weiss nichts von seiner eigenen. [He who knows nothing of foreign languages, knows nothing of his own.]* —
> Johann Wolfgang von Goethe (1749-1832)

On the surface this seems an insightful quote, and its relationship to social diversity seems to me, and hopefully to you, obvious enough. But situate this quote in any part of our current miasma of debates on diversity, and watch how quickly the whole enterprise becomes imbued with lexical melancholy.

Understanding the Misunderstanding

First, at least one astute observer will point out, very quickly and usually without having read the actual quote, that Goethe belongs to a category of historical figures known as DWMs: that is, Dead White Males (not to be confused with WMDs). This is done to reveal or "expose" my ostensible bias toward and preference for the (presumed) superiority of Western ways of thought and Western ideas of civilization, all of which are assumed, erroneously so, to be White. In doing so, I allegedly reveal an implicit or even explicit type of racism based on the fact that I did *not* choose something else, though many other choices might have been available. I could have drawn on Sanskrit poets, or Sufi theologians, or African visionaries, or Asian philosophers, but I did not do so, it is assumed, because either I do not know any of these other possibilities, which makes me culturally ignorant, or I do know them but dismiss them as inherently inferior to Goethe, which makes me culturally arrogant. The final piece of evidence for the case against me comes from the fact that I, like Goethe, am a White Male—not yet Dead, thankfully—but still, with two out of three counts against me in the DWM criminal code, it is enough at least for a cultural misdemeanor. What this means is that whatever I may have to say after this can be dismissed and rejected, largely on the grounds that as a white male, I clearly "don't get it." And if I have to ask the question of what exactly "it" is that I am supposed to get, this only shows how much of "it" I don't get.

Next, yet another observer will scrutinize the translation I have offered and point out, usually with a strange combination of glee and bile, that I have used the male pronoun *he* as a stand-in for humanity, revealing my witting or unwitting participation in the historical project to perpetuate and preserve the practice of patriarchy. There are various things I could offer here in my defense. Unlike German, for instance, English does not have a gender-neutral pronoun, and so historically authors have used *he* to mean anyone (I'll talk more about pronoun politics in a later chapter). I understand the argument that this predisposes readers to think normatively of men as actors, but consider the alternatives. I could have used *she*, but this is only a reversal of the original problem that to my mind actually strengthens the normative impact it seeks to undermine by calling attention to its syntactical nemesis. I could have used *he* in the first part and she in the second, which might be seen as a triumphant effort to place Goethe in the transgender community, but which could also be argued to be an mischievous act of witty phrasing or an unforgivable act of poor editing. I could also have used a plural pronoun in English, because due to a wonderful act of linguistic evolution we become neutered, or at least de-gendered, when we become plural (which interestingly is why some people like this pronoun). That would give us a different translation: "Those who do not know foreign languages, know nothing of their own." Better in terms of gender fairness, but now I will have the German academic community on my back for mistranslating Goethe, and the thought of being hounded day and night by German scholars who specialize in Goethe studies is almost *schrecklich* unbearable. Either way, I am once again in dubious circumstances, where my potential audience is spending more time finding any excuse to dismiss what I may have to say, rather than to listen, ponder, and act.

Lastly—as if the twin accusations of being a racist and a male chauvinist weren't enough—there would be still others who would point out the inherent elitism in the quote from Goethe and in my decision to choose that quote. One might point to my decision to include the original German language version of the quote: is this not an arrogant act of ivory tower intellectualism designed to ridicule those who do not know German? Another might point to the inference made by Goethe—that we should all be learning at least one foreign language—and point out that only those with sufficient leisure time and adequate financial resources could engage in such an undertaking, and therefore Goethe is crafting an ideal that is unobtainable for all except those at the upper echelons of society. By quoting Goethe, I would therefore stand accused of being complicit in an act of elitism. And once my message has been characterized as elitist, again, it could and probably would be dismissed as inappropriate for and inapplicable to the non-elites of mainstream society.

So there it is: one sentence into a discussion on diversity, and my introductory quote has caused three groups of people—those who think I am a racist, a sexist, or an elitist—to close their ears and their minds to anything else I might have to say. None of these accusations about my character is even remotely accurate, in spite of what my friends may say, but such is the nature of the dialogue on diversity than any defense of my actions or of my choices is already a fruitless exercise fraught with aggravation. But look what has happened: we have drifted hopelessly far away from the very idea embedded in the quote from Goethe, a quote that asks us to understand something different, something foreign, something unfamiliar, so that we may better understand ourselves and better understand others. We have quickly decayed from a plea to understand ourselves among others into a situation in which no one understands anything at all and no one *wants* to understand. The conversation becomes awkward, then uncomfortable, and then goes completely silent, an odd conclusion for a discussion that started with a plea for understanding. The sad irony is that more energy has been put into finding reasons to reject the message rather than to contemplate its meaning. We can't speak openly and we can't speak candidly. And that, in a nutshell, is what is wrong with diversity.

What's Good about Diversity?
When the US Supreme Court issued its ruling in *Schuette v. Coalition to Defend Affirmative Action* in April 2014, it in essence

upheld an earlier precedent that fundamentally changed the way the law looked at affirmative action.[3] Yes, *Schuette* upheld a ban on race-based preferences put in place in Michigan in 2006, but the reasoning through which it did so was less about the policy of affirmative action and more about the concept of diversity itself. In June 2003, the US Supreme Court issued its ruling in the landmark case of *Grutter v. Bollinger,* one of many cases that have tried to challenge various aspects of legally-mandated diversity policies such as affirmative action programs.[4] What makes *Grutter* different and special is that it is the only one to have its holding (a fancy legal term for the ruling) anchored in the concept that diversity is an inherent good, one that needs no justification or explanation. The court was split on the ruling in what is the judicial equivalent of a 7-10 split in bowling: the court ruled in a 5-4 decision that the University of Michigan's affirmative action program, designed to obtain what was called a "critical mass" of racially diverse students through preferential admissions policies, was *not* unconstitutional and did not violate the Fourteenth Amendment (guaranteeing equality before the law). The most concise way to summarize the reasoning behind the ruling is to say that the Court believed that creating a racially diverse entering class to the University of Michigan Law School served a "compelling interest" (to have diversity) and also satisfied the requirements of "strict scrutiny" in that the program was narrowly tailored to achieve the specific and desired end (diversity). The Court assumed that diversity is an inherent good, though at no point does the Court explain precisely

---

[3] Full text can be found at: https://www.supremecourt.gov/opinions/13pdf/12-682_8759.pdf

[4] Full text can be found at: https://www.law.cornell.edu/supct/html/02-241.ZX1.html

why or how this is so. Diversity is good, and it just *is* good. No explanation was apparently necessary.

Now, the justices of the Supreme Court, regardless of their political leanings, are all intelligent and eloquent people, each in their own way, so this lack of explanation is not a matter of mere oversight. While there are numerous references to the elements of diversity, particularly in the majority opinion that carried the ruling of the court, and while the legal argument is replete with relatively persuasive legal reasoning, the part about *why* diversity is good is not argued but rather assumed. Since I think one of the greatest flaws in nearly all of the discussions and debates over diversity is that they assume what they ought to explain, it is worth taking a closer look at this particular ruling. This is as true for the majority opinion as it is for the dissenting (minority) opinions, particularly since the dissent is sometimes quite bitter and acerbic.

The majority opinion, authored by Justice Sandra Day O'Connor, consisted of two elements, one legal and the other philosophical. The legal element consisted of a process of legal reasoning that requires some explanation, especially for those who opted not to experience the blissful joy of law school (and by blissful I mean painful). The case originated out of a challenge made by Barbara Grutter, an aspiring applicant to the University of Michigan Law School. The claim made by Ms. Grutter was that the University of Michigan had no "compelling interest" to justify the use of race as a predominant determining factor in its admissions policy in order to strengthen its efforts to create a diverse class of entering students. If race were used in this way, Ms. Grutter claimed, it would amount to a quota system in which a specific number of seats were reserved for persons from designated racial groups (or other targeted identity groups, though race is the focus of the case), a practice that was struck down and ruled unconstitutional in a previous landmark Supreme Court case, *Regents of the Univ. of California v. Bakke* (1978). For something to serve as a compelling interest, it must be something that is considered necessary or essential, and not just desirable or preferable, for the proper and just functioning of the polity it serves. If the interest is deemed necessary or essential—and the majority opinion in *Grutter* stated that diversity was just such a thing—then it must also satisfy two other requirements: first, it must be achieved through a policy design that is narrowly tailored (and not broadly construed) to achieve precisely the desired outcome—in this case to create a diverse entering class—and second, it must be articulated through the least restrictive means possible.

In the *Bakke* case, which struck down what was in essence a quota system to guarantee specific racial and ethnic groups a reserved number of slots in the entering class, these requirements were not satisfied. In *Grutter*, however, the majority opinion argued that the admissions process at the University of Michigan was *not* a quota system since it used race only as a potential "plus" factor, an element that could be considered if necessary, and only alongside other qualifications, accomplishments, and achievements of law school applicants. In other words, the University of Michigan would consider race only as an ancillary element in creating what it described as a necessary "critical mass" of diversity at the law school.

The central component that made *Grutter* the landmark case it was in relation to diversity, however, was its justification in rendering the obtainment of diversity a compelling interest. All previous cases before the Court that challenged one or more aspects of existing affirmative action programs had used the argument that addressing and rectifying past historical injustices against specific racial and ethnic groups was a compelling interest. The *Bakke* ruling, for instance, did not question the need for affirmative action policies but rather focused on the sloppy and ill-conceived manner in which the University of California system sought to apply its affirmative action agenda. In *Grutter*, the Court shifted away from the idea of offering redress and remedy for past historical injustices and instead based its majority opinion on the idea that diversity itself was an inherent good and therefore represented a legitimate compelling interest. The Court claimed essentially that diversity was just a good thing in general and, since an educational institution was involved in the case, a good thing for the environment of learning at all levels of matriculation in the United States. Diversity had been removed from history and transferred to the realm of philosophy: diversity was defensibly good, it was eternally good, it was effectively good, and it was inherently good.

The majority opinion therefore deferred to the claim of the University of Michigan that crafting diversity in the classroom is central to the educational mission in the United States, and that diversity in and of itself—which incidentally is never actually defined in the opinion—would yield educational benefits that are, in the words of the Court, "substantial." Simply being exposed to a classroom and an academic environment that has been carefully designed to have sufficient diversity, the court argued, would enhance cross-racial understanding, would dismantle racial stereotypes and therefore the racism they create, and would lead to a more "robust exchange of ideas" in the process of education. The court did not stop there. It extended the benefits of diversity into the broader spectrum of American life, stating that diversity was essential to the future effectiveness of the US armed forces and hence was a cornerstone of American security; that diversity was essential to the future productivity of the American workplace and hence was a foundation for the American economy; that diversity was essential to the future vibrancy of civil society and civic life and hence was a pillar of American democracy. These claims may indeed be true, but they were strangely presented in the majority opinion as self-evidently true, without any accompanying explanation as to how one necessarily led to the other. And with my own experience and background in higher education, I could not help but wonder as I read the majority opinion: if these are self-evident truths, and diversity is an inherent and obvious good, why is it one of the most divisive and contentious topics in American life? And why are American educational institutions replete with resentment and acrimony, among faculty and students, every time the issue of diversity rears its complicated head?

Diversity under question and on time
Some of the reasons as to why diversity is never as straightforward as it seems can be found in the dissenting opinions to *Grutter*. Justice Kennedy, for instance, wrote in his dissenting opinion that the Court had confused the explanation of an educational objective (to create diversity) with the means by which that objective was obtained; just because diversity was inherently good did not mean that any means designed to achieve it were therefore also good. In other words, diversity could not and should not be achieved "by any means necessary." Justice Kennedy also pointed out that racial preferences can be "the most divisive of all policies," even to the point where they can "destroy confidence in the Constitution and the idea of equality." In spite of the claims of the University of Michigan that any effort to dismantle or restrict the policies designed to create this critical mass of diversity would have disastrous consequences for the future of the university and for the law school in particular, all of the dissenting opinions pointed out that the percentage of students admitted from targeted racial and ethnic groups differed very little from the years before the diversity-enhancing admissions policy was implemented to the years after. Chief Justice Rehnquist, joined by Justices Scalia, Kennedy, and Thomas, wrote that the numbers themselves made little sense, as the percentages of each of the targeted groups that were admitted lacked any defensible consistency or any rational explanation that could be used to justify the putative critical mass of diversity that

the university championed. Justice Kennedy went so far as to call the idea of a critical mass a "delusion."

In a separate dissenting opinion, Justice Scalia wrote the shortest and—this was Justice Scalia after all—the most predictably scathing indictment of the whole enterprise of diversity as construed by the University of Michigan. For Scalia, approaching diversity in the way that the University of Michigan had done would lead only to "tribalism" and the dissolution of American civil society. The University of Michigan, at least according to Scalia, was simply offering rewards to students for separating themselves from each other and from the rest of American society. In Scalia's view, a view that resonates collectively in all of the dissenting opinions, diversity was not a unifying but a disintegrative process, at least as currently practiced, and the majority opinion of the Court, in sanctioning a program that in the minority's opinion did not satisfy the criteria for strict scrutiny (and hence was unconstitutional), had done a disservice to the law and to the very fabric of American society. The Court, as it turns out, was as divided among itself as was the society and the polity for whom it was designed to render justice. No matter where diversity shows up, it tends to divide far more than it unifies. Something must clearly be very wrong.

There are a few final observations about this case that I can offer to illustrate why the current discourse on diversity in American society is such a difficult and awkward conversation to have. Indeed, we don't enjoy the conversation on diversity as much as we endure it. One of the things that even the majority opinion of the Court in *Grutter* agreed upon was that the diversity program of the University of Michigan, and by extension all such programs in the United States, was to be necessarily of limited duration and *not* a permanent part of American law or society. The court stated that if these types of programs were of any substantive and justifiable benefit in the present, then part of that justification included a provision that they should be entirely unnecessary in the near future, offering the surprisingly specific time frame of *twenty-five years*. In other words, the Supreme Court was acknowledging the polarizing effects that diversity policies often have—at one point calling them "dangerous"—and was claiming that the pain and discomfort of the present could only be justified by the realized substantive benefits they would produce in the (near) future. In making this claim, the Supreme Court was falling into line with current standards of international human rights law, where foundational treaties such as the *International Covenant on the Elimination of All Forms of Racial Discrimination* (ICERD) state that affirmative action programs designed to benefit one or more specific targeted groups do not violate other human rights principles of equality for all before the law *provided that such programs are of limited duration*. What this means specifically in the context of the *Grutter* decision is that, according to the Supreme Court, diversity should be and must be achieved within one generation, and that generation is this generation. In other words, this generation is the last generation we have to get diversity right. Either we succeed or we fail, and we have twenty-five years, with the clock starting in 2003 (the year of the ruling), to figure out which it will be. Right now, we're over half-way there, chronologically speaking, but in terms of diversity itself, we're hopelessly behind schedule. Things don't look good.

On a final note, the Court also made clear what type of society the policies and programs of diversity should create in this twenty-five year window of opportunity. In specific and unambiguous language, the Court argued that diversity policies should aim to create "one Nation" that is colorblind, integrated, and most importantly, "indivisible." In spite of the clarity of the Court on this point, there is considerable disagreement on what type of policies and what type of programs should be implemented to make this happen, in one generation no less. To some ears, it sounds like a twenty-five-year agenda to create an integrated and assimilated society, and diversity should be working to do just that—assimilate and integrate. To others, it sounds like a warning that we need to call attention to and acknowledge our differences first, before we can attain an indivisible American society, and so diversity in the present should focus on highlighting our differences rather than trying to cover them up. Either way, it is all an exuberant mess.

Learning and unlearning diversity
One of the other important things that emerges out of *Grutter* is the centrality of education and especially higher education in the larger project of attaining diversity. Diversity, it seems, is something we learn, at least for now or at least for the next twenty-five years. What could be wrong with that, you might ask? Well, for starters, one of the secret or perhaps not-so-secret aspects of institutions of higher learning in the United States is that they are heavily populated by some of the smartest stupid people, or stupidest smart people, in the world. Contrast, for instance, the idealistic comment in *Grutter* about how diversity enhances the "robust exchange of ideas" at the university with the following example of how discussions about diversity actually take place at the university. In Justice Kennedy's dissenting opinion, he notes how the former Dean of Admissions at the University of Michigan Law School had described in his testimony to the Court how faculty had debated on whether or not Cubans could be considered Hispanics. The answer offered by one faculty member to this already absurd question upped the ante in the stupid pot by arguing that Cubans—presumably Cuban-Americans though it was not made clear in the original statement—could not be considered Hispanics because Cubans are Republicans. If you read that sentence and felt some of your brain cells suddenly atrophy and die, I feel your pain. Many of the problems and much of the acrimony associated with diversity stem not from a general antipathy towards the idea itself but more

with the idiocy and lunacy that accompany the idea on its checkered journey into the world of reality.

Though clearly there are exceptions, universities in general in the United States tend to be seen as institutions with liberal proclivities, with some departments making efforts to compete among themselves for labels like "most progressive" or even "most radical," much like high-schoolers compete for meaningless awards like "most congenial" or "nicest hair" or "least likely to harm kittens." Like the awards from high-school, these academic labels are mostly useless and are poor indicators of, well, anything. Many academics are well-known for their vociferous advocacy for policies that promote enhanced diversity at the university and in other institutions of public life, usually arguing that sacrifices must be made for the greater good of society and usually arguing in language that aspires to noble rhetoric but achieves only curmudgeonly prattle. Nevertheless, if you look closely at who is engaging in this type of advocacy for diversity, you will quickly discover that those who are calling most loudly for sacrifice are those who are most likely to be immune from having to make any such sacrifice themselves. Yep, it's the tenured faculty who call for sacrifice, because they know that the sacrifice is not theirs to make. Once a faculty member at a university obtains tenure, short of bludgeoning a student to death right in the classroom, there are very few things that allow a university to remove them (note that boring students to death in the classroom does not affect tenure at all). And even then, the university would prefer to let the professor-turned-bludgeoner offer a new course on something like Behavioral Aspects of Personal Bludgeoning rather than actually terminate his or her employment. In other words, there is a distinct hollowness to most of the radical advocacy found in our universities.

If you want to watch the rhetoric change instantaneously from radical advocacy for to staunch opposition against diversity, all you need to do is make the simple suggestion that in the interest of speeding up the attainment of diversity at institutions of higher learning, tenured faculty will have their tenure retroactively withdrawn and their employment (and pensions and benefits) terminated, in order to open up more tenured faculty positions for underrepresented ethnic and racial groups. If ever there were to be a riot among senior faculty, complete with torn tufts of frayed tweed and drifting clouds of multicolored chalk dust—and I know such an image unsettles the soul—it would be over the possibility that those advocating sacrifice for diversity would actually have to make that sacrifice themselves. Several years ago, Pulitzer Prize-winning historian James M. MacPherson wrote a short essay in *Perspectives*, a publication of the American Historical Association, in which he offered his support for racial preferences in academic hiring.[5] What was peculiar about the essay was the reasoning: he himself, he confessed in the essay, had received his academic position through the "old boys network" and had enjoyed continued success throughout his career as a result. But now, however, he understands that it was wrong to have done so, and so universities should utilize racial preferences to rectify these past injustices. At no point does he offer to resign his position or pay back his ill-gotten but substantial salary. Instead, it is the next generation or other, untenured faculty—pretty much anyone else—who should accept career sacrifices for mistakes that he knowingly made himself. One of the major problems of diversity is that somehow it is always someone else's problem, someone else's sacrifice to make. When diversity advocates claim that sacrifices must be made in the name of diversity, what they really mean is that *other* people must make sacrifices. Before we can attain a diversity that works, we have to own it ourselves—all of us. We cannot ask others to make sacrifices that we ourselves are not willing to make.

---

5 James M. McPherson, "Deconstructing Affirmative Action," *Perspectives* 41:4 (April 2003)

Aside from tenured faculty, there is at least one other group at the university that actively advocates expanding the presence of diversity at the university: faculty who would personally benefit from diversity programs, by which I mean recently-minted PhD graduates entering the academic job market. I will have more to say on how educational institutions approach and distort diversity in a later chapter, but for now, let me briefly explain the academic job market in order to show how the promotion of diversity, again usually in lofty and noble rhetoric, is often disingenuous and frequently corrupt.

Unlike normal job markets where job openings appear on a continuous basis, in the academic world, there is only one application season per year in which potential candidates can apply for an academic post. Universities list their openings, finishing or recently-finished doctoral students apply for these positions, and though candidates can apply for as many positions as they wish, the applications and interviews all happen around the same time of year. Unsuccessful applicants therefore have to wait for the following year to try again, which means scrambling to find some kind of temporary employment to hold them over until the next season. After about three application seasons at most, universities usually lose interest and consider such candidates unhireable. What this means is that anyone looking for a job in the academic world needs to gain any advantage they can, and for many candidates, claiming "diversity" has become their best asset for two interrelated reasons. One, unlike academic ideas, which can be challenged and disputed, diversity as an asset is an absolute—if there are ten applicants, but only five are from what are called "underrepresented" groups, then the competition is instantly cut by fifty percent. The second reason works in conjunction with the first: universities are under constant pressure to increase diversity—it isn't a coincidence that all of the major court cases involving affirmative action come from universities—and being able to present yourself as a candidate

Understanding the Misunderstanding

who can "add diversity" helps academic search committees cut their work significantly by considering only candidates who are "diverse." If you don't know what it means to be "diverse," don't worry—universities don't either, and even the Supreme Court couldn't or wouldn't spell it out in precise terms. But to put it in blunt and colloquial language, at least in the university environment, and in most other places as well, to be "diverse" is to be from a non-white minority group, to be a woman, or to be both.

In a later chapter I will discuss in more detail why these strategies actually undermine diversity and jeopardize whatever benefits diversity is intended to produce. But for now, the short answer is this: if diversity is a project that is designed to help us understand other people, how is that supposed to happen when the primary strategy is to promote only ourselves? That is, diversity is almost always promoted in the interest of the self, and not in the interest of understanding or promoting someone else. You will never hear, for example, a black male candidate for a job tell their potential employer in an interview that they should hire more Asian women. That's someone else's diversity, and someone else's diversity is a threat, another competitive voice in the arena of diversity-based self-promotion. Sometimes, as with the academic job market, diversity is invoked as a personal strategy. At other times, it is a type of self-directed advocacy based on "membership" in the specific identity group to which a person subscribes. Instead of asking society to make a sacrifice for the greater good, diversity becomes a way to pass that sacrifice on to some other person or some other group, usually in the hopes of benefitting from their loss or their sacrifice. My group wants more, so your group will have to accept less.

Sadly, and again I will discuss this in more detail in a later chapter—right now we are just easing ourselves into the discussion—these tactics are often passed on to students, who are inculcated in the classroom or in various other forms of peer-to-peer identity-based activism to accept this puerile behavior as the "way things are." I spend a good deal of time with my undergraduate students, helping them prepare for the transition to post-university life. In many of these interactions, such as helping them to craft an effective law-school application, I am continuously surprised by how many of them have no compunction at all about "playing the race card" (and I'm not putting words into their mouths, since they are the ones who use that phrase—they are well aware what they are doing) if it will help them get into a better law school or a higher-paying job. One Filipino-American student brought a draft of his personal essay for his law school application to me for some feedback, and the essay began with the following sentence: "I believe that my diversity will make me an ideal candidate for your law school…" I thought that seemed a very strange way to begin the essay, and so I asked him why he thought that would be the best way to make the all-important first impression for his law school application. What he told me was that he had read the personal statements of other "students of color" (more on that label later) who had been admitted to top law schools and who had posted their essays online to show other students of color the right things to say—the "tricks," so to speak—to get into a good law school. Particularly at a time when an increasing number of law suits and legal challenges had emerged opposing the use of race as a factor in determining admissions—Proposition 209, which passed in California in 1996, had prohibited public universities and other public institutions from considering race, ethnicity, or gender in admissions or employment decisions—the use of "diversity" in an application became code for "non-white." So in an application where the applicant stated that they were "diverse," and also stated that they had worked for a group like Justice for Filipinos (for example), any law school could make an educated guess that the applicant was most likely Filipino or Filipino-American, and therefore could find a way to continue to consider race and ethnicity without ever having to mention race or

Understanding the Misunderstanding

ethnicity. Diversity had become code for race, and specifically, for any race other than white.

The problem with these attitudes and practices is that they amount to a misguided strategy to gain something in the short-run that makes everyone lose something in the long-run. The deeper these attitudes and practices sink into institutions of higher learning, the more difficult it becomes to imagine an America where in twenty-five years—the time frame specified by the Supreme Court in *Grutter*—we will have attained any sort of meaningful or substantive type of diversity. Higher education has failed to teach diversity as an inclusive and integrative ideal, and what students have learned is how to use diversity to obtain benefits for themselves without concern for the expense it transfers to others. The situation is such a mess that I would argue that we actually need to *unlearn* diversity, at least the way it is currently packaged and promoted, and learn it again anew through a complete reconstruction of the intellectual architecture of our educational institutions. Diversity is supposed to be a process through which we learn to understand ourselves *among* others. Instead, as it is currently practiced, it has become a politicized and perverted process of promoting ourselves *against* others.

The awkward silence in the room: talking diversity
As if the attempts to create a vibrant and viable form of diversity were not fraught with enough problems, there is the additional problem embedded in the whole enterprise that the ongoing conversation about diversity gets pruned down more and more, down to the point when it becomes little more than a continuously awkward silence. If there is one thing we need to do most to get diversity back on track, it is to be able to talk openly and honestly—even to the point of saying things that might be embarrassing to ourselves or offensive to others—so at least we have the full range of ideas and opinions at our disposal when we start the reconstruction. But

this we simply do not have, not yet and not now. In a society that can possibly claim the strongest right to freedom of speech in the world, we lamentably have a situation where, at least when it comes to diversity, everyone is simply afraid to speak. We *could* speak, but we choose not to. We are afraid to.[6] All of the sensitivity that has allegedly emerged as a result of years of diversity talk has produced only a truncated conversation at best. Questioning any aspect of diversity will usually bring the ugly charge of racism into the air, which vitiates the possibility of any further understanding as the conversation collapses into counterproductive questions of who is or is not a racist, instead of fruitful questions of what diversity can or cannot do. Rather than cultivating an environment of mutual understanding, we have only an environment of fear and loathing. We stew in our own internal monologues, and diversity seems to be only a bitter rumor, a false promise, or an urban legend. Nothing more.

Consider, for instance, how often the word "phobia" is invoked in any discussion of diversity or identity. I will have much more to say on this in a later chapter, but for now, take a moment to think of how powerful an act this is in shutting down any further debate or dialog or understanding. It becomes the answer to the question for which there is no answer. Do you think that homosexuality might be a choice? You are homophobic. Do you wonder if Muslim women are required to wear a headscarf? You are Islamophobic. Rather than provide an answer, the very act of asking the question is transformed into the problem. And the only way to solve that problem is to stop asking questions. The discussion is over before it starts. It has become, as the Supreme Court justices affirmed

---

6 For an example from Australia, see Nigel Bunyan, "Racism fears 'left Asian gang free to rape girls'," *The Sydney Morning Herald* (May 9, 2012) at http://www.smh.com.au/world/racism-fears-left-asian-gang-free-to-rape-girls-20120509-1ycfu.html

in the *Grutter* decision, something too "dangerous" to talk about. How are we going to have sufficient diversity in twenty-five years, to the point where we will no longer need any specialized programs such as affirmative action, if in the present we cannot even talk to each other about it? So much fear and hostility suffuse the air, and all we have become are mutes who try to scream at the deaf.

The conversation is distorted in many other ways as well. In some cases, connections that would provide a new perspective to shift the diversity debate back to something more constructive are simply rejected out of hand. These connections or alternative perspectives are rejected largely because they create an environment for a renegotiation of the prominent but very stale style of argument of you-are-perpetrator-and-I-am-victim that dominates most of the conversations that circulate around diversity. At a lecture I attended a few years back, on the topic of the self-hating violence that women inflict on their bodies to conform, as the speaker argued, to the patriarchal desires of men, one man in the audience raised the question, after the lecture was finished, of whether men's unrealistic expectations of women's appearances were similar to women's unrealistic expectation of men's appearances. The man, who had thinning hair and a sharply receding hairline, made a few observations about how people feel it is acceptable to make fun of bald men, and how women in general associate manhood and sexiness with having a "full head of hair."[7] The man then asked if a man's desire for large breasts in a woman, for instance, was any different than a woman's desire for a headful of hair on a man. The professor giving the lecture, who was a woman, became visibly angry and shot back sarcastically that she was sorry that the man was "follicle challenged" (leading to chuckles and claps of delight

---

7 For a related example of this, see "Bald teacher loses disabled claim," *BBC News* (April 16, 2008) at http://news.bbc.co.uk/2/hi/uk_news/scotland/tayside_and_central/7350523.stm

from the audience) but found it ludicrous that the two situations could be compared. Men had power, said the woman, and women didn't, and so when men underwent bodily transformations it was to "exert more power," but when women did the same, it was due to "male oppression."

Now, I will admit that I do not know the personal history of the man who asked the question, and I will also admit that the comparison would need a bit of fine-tuning for a serious investigation. But I did become intrigued in that moment as to why the woman giving the lecture had to reject the parallel connection out of hand, as something that just couldn't be. Baldness, after all, like gender, skin color, body shape, and many other elements of identity associated with diversity, is caused by genetics. Men with male pattern baldness are born that way, as the saying goes, and men spend millions of dollars trying to cover up or prevent baldness largely due to the stereotypical expectations of what constitutes a "real man." Seriously, can you think of any male model for Ralph Lauren or Calvin Klein who is balding? In an era when we are celebrating plus-sized female models and are normatively encouraged to see women of all shapes and sizes as equally beautiful, I'll await the day when plus-sized, balding men are walking the runways modeling Calvin Klein underwear and women are oohing and aahing over how hot they are. Of course, that day won't ever happen, because what women want to see are men with full heads of hair and perfectly-sculpted bodies, an appearance that remains impossible for the vast majority of men.

I'm not suggesting that hair loss in men is somehow the equivalent of gender persecution or the entire history of patriarchy. But I think the connection is at least worth considering and discussing. Perhaps a woman who wants to wear heels to attract a man is not all that different from a man who wants to grow hair to attract a woman. But in the context of this particular lecture, the mere possibility could not be entertained. The connection was soundly and rudely rejected largely because it complicated and undermined the rather simplistic perspective that had been presented in the lecture. Do women put themselves through tremendous discomfort and pain for men? Absolutely. But why is it so dangerous an idea to suggest that men might be doing something similar for women? There will be much more to say about gender and diversity later, but for now, hold that thought.

Another interesting and more provocative parallel connection that is often made—and just as quickly rejected by proponents of diversity—comes from an organization that makes many people cringe with discomfort or gesticulate with whelps of disdain: PETA (as in, People for the Ethical Treatment of Animals). A few years ago, PETA had initiated a campaign on college campuses around the country, including my home institution, the University of California, Berkeley, to highlight animal cruelty and exploitation. The campaign consisted of large displays that presented images of black slaves in various forms of shackles and constraints, sometimes subjected to painful forms of punishment and abuse, which were then positioned side-by-side with images of animals in similar shackles and restraints, and also subjected to variety of painful forms of abuse, such as medical experimentation or cosmetic testing.[8] The display was accompanied by quotes from a variety of people, including slavery abolitionists and former slaves, that suggested parallels between the exploitative treatment of slaves in the past and the exploitative treatment of animals in the present. What the display was suggesting was that systematic forms of violence, regardless of the object of that violence (whether human or nonhuman), follow a similar pattern. All are generated by socially-embedded belief systems that make such violence acceptable and tolerable through the articulation of hierarchies based on

---

[8] For a similar campaign, see https://www.peta.org/blog/new-tv-ad-are-you-supporting-the-modern-day-slave-trade/

difference. Among animals, for instance, we consider dogs to be cute and cuddly but cows to be slow and stupid, which is why killing dogs evokes horror and killing cows evokes dinner. The whole point of the display was to show that these hierarchies are socially-constructed and not scientifically-justified—that is, they are created precisely to justify systematic exploitation and to make what is unpalatable more palatable to the society that carries out such forms of injurious action—which means that the key to ending all systematic forms of violence and exploitation is to change the way society thinks.

Though the larger point that PETA was trying to make was to stop animal exploitation and abuse, I will admit that I was quite interested in the way the suggestions made by the display directly related to the idea of diversity, which is at its root a massive project to change the way that American society thinks about and considers various forms of difference in human identities. PETA was pushing the debate outside the box by asking whether we should also consider the meaning of difference beyond the species boundary. Indeed, PETA was suggesting that racial boundaries and hierarchies were created in ways very similar to the boundaries and hierarchies we hold between species (creating a parallel between *racism* and what is often called *speciesism*). But what interested me more than anything was the immediate and angry reaction by student groups on campus, and in particular by those who spend so much of their time promoting diversity. African-American student groups in particular expressed outrage because they claimed that the display was trying to show that African-Americans were animals, and that therefore PETA and its agenda were both racist. I was quite flabbergasted by these claims against PETA, because quite frankly they were so utterly nonsensical. If I claim that a woman deserves the same rights as a man, for instance, I am not claiming that a woman *is* a man. If I claim that homosexuals have an equal right to marry as heterosexuals, I am not claiming that gay people are straight. As with the question in the lecture on women's desire to conform to male desires, I was drawn to the idea of why PETA's suggestion was so threatening to these various student groups, and why they moved so quickly to reject these new ideas or characterize them as laughably absurd or patently offensive. Progressives often become haplessly conservative when confronted with ideas more progressive than their own.

The key to this situation lies in the way that challenges such as those made by the PETA campaign alter the debate on diversity. The debate on diversity often takes the form of a contest between different groups to move the debate and the policies it generates into a position that will provide maximum benefits for the group or groups advocating change. As I stated previously, much of the rhetoric and activism that constitutes the ongoing talk on diversity is self-directed and not other-directed. Once the debate is successfully moved into a position that provides specific benefits, a process that is often referred to as *empowerment*, there is a tremendous reluctance to allow the debate to change, a reluctance that is often depicted somewhat heroically as *resistance*. Change almost always occurs as a result of the introduction of new information that alters the current perspective, and so the easiest way to prevent change is to reject new information, especially if that new information jeopardizes the benefits produced or accrued, or allows those benefits to flow to some other, now newly-empowered group. To suggest that men may respond to expectations of women in a manner similar to the way that women respond to the expectations of men, or to suggest that systems of slavery may have something in common with patterns of animal mistreatment, is to shift the debate in new directions that allow for new possibilities and novel renegotiations of the parameters of the debate. But moments of transition such as these, though potentially quite liberating for everyone, threaten the power of those who seek to maintain things as they are. In this sense, the "radical" debates on diversity end up mirroring and mimicking the initial refusal even to entertain the idea of diversity by the "old boys networks" of a generation ago. The revolutionaries of today are already the reactionaries of tomorrow.

If part of the failure of the debate on diversity to lead to the results it promises stems from the rejection of connections that could open up or at least reinvigorate that debate, another part of the failure comes from the tendency to create and entrench connections that are not really there. Several years ago, for instance, at a dinner party I attended, a Latino couple were talking about racism and proceeded to narrate an anecdote about what had happened to them at a local hospital just the day before. They had gone to a hospital in Oakland, and were upset at the treatment they received at the clinic where they had an appointment. They had been treated rudely upon arrival by the receptionist, who was a white woman. Because they felt they had been treated brusquely or dismissively, with an attitude that made the couple feel that the receptionist considered them too stupid to know simple things, the conclusion was that she was "clearly racist." The whole incident happened because she was white and they were Latino, which then led to a more general claim of how America is "such a racist country." The only problem with the story is this: I use the same hospital, and I knew exactly the woman whom they were talking about, because the same receptionist had been rude to me as well. In fact, she had been rude to everyone, regardless of color, at least as far as I could tell from my experiences waiting to be called for my appointment. But for my dinner guests, it was all filtered through the prism of racism. When Whites meet Whites, rudeness is rudeness, but when Latinos meet Whites, rudeness is racism. But the connection between rude treatment and racism can be a false one. In my dinner conversation, what was really an incident of rudeness had been mistaken for an incident of racism. If diversity cannot help us tell the difference between rudeness and racism, then we have a very serious problem on our hands.

Again, we reach the question of why—why would this couple, or anyone else for that matter, want to interpret every social interaction through the lens of racism? The answer emerges, again, from the way the debate on diversity is currently framed. If diversity is seen as a project designed to correct historical injustice, then filtering everything through the lens of racism provides a compelling narrative for the type of systematic injustice that allows someone to make a legitimate claim to be a recipient of the benefits of diversity-based policies. If diversity is seen as a project to create social environments which are characterized by a multiplicity of ethnic and racial backgrounds, a shift seen clearly in the *Grutter* decision, then filtering everything through the lens of racism provides an ongoing litany of examples of being denied access to these social environments, or being mistreated in them, which again allows someone to make a legitimate claim to receive the benefits of diversity-based policies. In other words, the discourse on diversity creates every incentive to interpret every life-event in terms of racism, specifically as a victim of racism, and absolutely no incentive to see it in any other way. Our current version of diversity actually encourages us to make America as racist as possible, because the more racism we can allege, the more benefits we can demand.

The problem with this tendency is that it actually weakens and cheapens the charge of racism when and where it happens, and yes, it does happen, and far more often than it should (ideally, it should never happen). The overuse of the claim of racism, much like the overuse of the claim of genocide, ends up creating a credibility gap as it becomes increasingly difficult to sort through and separate *substantive* claims of racism from *convenient* claims of racism. Nothing weakens the impact of seeing the true ugliness of racism like turning it into a caricature of itself. This approach to diversity also divides the population into those who are victims and those who are not: it creates a divide between receivers and givers, between beneficiaries and sacrificers, that becomes nearly impossible to broach and nearly impossible to resolve. People who question diversity are "privileged," while those who demand it are "victims," with both categories about as nuanced as a shotgun blast in a Zen garden. If diversity is supposed to create an integrated and unified society, then once again, we have a serious problem on our hands.

Diversity and (the lack of) dignity
Somehow—and I will explain how in the rest of this book—the conversation about diversity, which was supposed to create understanding and empathy, has instead created fear, antagonism, suspicion, and cynicism. Although years of diversity-based activism and mobilization have made the issue more prominent on college campuses and other institutions around the country, the conversations that have emerged out of this have not been anything close to what the original intent might have been. When a job search is conducted, for instance—whether in academia or other fields of employment—even before a single application is received, even at the earliest point in the process when the job description is being written, discussion centers on questions such as whether this has to be a "diversity hire" and if so, what the target group should be. I am quite sure that anyone who has ever been on a job-search committee did two things when they read the previous sentence: one, they laughed cynically under their breath and whispered "that's so true," and two, they realized they had to say that under their breath because diversity in a job search is a bit like Fight Club, and as everyone knows, rule number one of Fight Club is that you never talk about Fight Club.[9]

---

9 For an example from the Bay Area, see Paul Roscelli, "Is Hiring Goal Diversity or Equality?" *SFGate* (March 28, 2000) at http://www.sfgate.com/opinion/openforum/article/Is-Hiring-Goal-Diversity-or-Equality-Job-2708127.php

Job descriptions are often custom-tailored in a strange, coded language that is meant to send subtle and sometimes not-so-subtle messages to elicit applications from preferred groups. In the academic world, for instance, departments will start rumors circulating—word magically gets out that "they are looking for a Latina"—although none of this is ever written down explicitly because, for obvious reasons, it would be illegal to run a search this way. Remember, it's Fight Club. The problem with these "diversity hires" is that everyone knows they are diversity hires, and a diversity hire is never seen the same as a normal hire. If a university department hires a gay Latino, for instance, you will hear people say things like "he's a twofer," meaning he checks off not one but two diversity boxes (gay *and* Latino). The reason that this is considered a good thing is not for the diversity it brings, but rather because fulfilling two diversity categories with one job search takes pressure off of the department or division and allows it much more leeway in the next job search. The attitude is that in the next job search, without the pressure of a having to make a "diversity hire," the department can focus on choosing someone based on talent rather than identity.

Not surprisingly, given the cynical if not demeaning way that diversity enters the employment dialogue, those who are hired as diversity hires often end up with a sense of alienation and separation from other colleagues. Such new hires end up starting their careers in the unenviable position of having to prove they have talent, that they were more than just a choice to "showcase diversity," and while some may succeed, most experience a losing battle and do their best to make a personal peace with a good job and a bad environment. It would be the easiest path to write this off as just one more example of deeply embedded racism that will eventually be eradicated through more and more diversity. But the more constructive interpretation, one that is central to the mission of this book, is that it is more accurately seen as a by-product of the flawed diversity-related practices and policies that we currently have, and the artificial and heavy-handed ways that diversity is shoved into institutions. More diversity won't fix this, but better diversity will. And that's what we're here to do—to craft a better diversity.

Shortchanging the robust exchange
To understand how the very discussion of diversity has become part of the problem, we can also peer into the veritable learning lab of diversity itself: the classroom. The stunted and truncated language of debates over diversity that we see in the world of "grown-ups" do not emerge out of thin air, but is forged, sharpened, and honed in the classrooms of our schools from one end of the country to the other. There are two parts to the classroom, one involving teacher-to-student pedagogy and the other involving the much undervalued (and much maligned) peer-to-peer transfer of knowledge. Both of these constitute the educational environment that is designed to help students prepare for the ineluctable transition into the grit and complexity of the real world. It is no secret that K-12 education in America has not done the finest job of preparing students for the disorienting sink-or-swim leap into the real world—and I should add that much of that problem is a funding failure rather than a teaching failure. But how does it fare in preparing students for higher education in the United States, for participation in life and study at college, that special environment singled out by the Supreme Court in the *Grutter* decision as invaluable to the future of diversity in America?

The classroom can and should be an arena where the "robust exchange of ideas" can circulate openly in an atmosphere of freedom of thought, conscience, and opinion. Yet when it comes to diversity, the same tendency to truncate the dialogue and reduce the conversation to an awkward silence that happens elsewhere happens here as well. The unnatural silence of the classroom should perhaps be more disconcerting than the awkward silence we find elsewhere, because if there is any place where we would expect to find an open and honest discussion, it is in the university classroom among spirited minds still thriving on the fertile soil of idealism and activism. But in my experience, this does not happen, and again, the reason comes down to the flawed nature of the debate on diversity itself.

In many my courses, one of the most common phrases I hear over and over again at the start of a question or comment is this: "As a person of color..." At some point in the peer-to-peer process of learning, and to a considerable extent in the formal teacher-to-student process as well, students from minority groups are taught that they are "invisible" to the majority, and hence calling attention to yourself primarily by signifying your minority identity is seen as an everyday form of activism to remedy the presumed blindness that collectively and equally afflicts everyone in the majority population of the country. By beginning a question or comment with a phrase like "As a person of color..." not only does the student call attention to their identity, but it primes the rest of the statement for the announcement that what follows should be heard as a special contribution to diversity, one that could never be provided by the people in the classroom who were born with a tragic absence of color. Unfortunately, what actually happens in these charged moments, far more often than not, is that once again, any meaningful dialog or any chance for mutual understanding is shut down or preempted by the use of this phrase. Here is how that happens.

There are several ways that the introduction of this simple phrase changes the classroom environment in a way that is deleterious to the promotion of diversity. First, there is the painfully awkward fact that most of the time, the second part of the sentence has nothing to do with being a person of color. "As a person of color, I think that racism is wrong." This statement does not really add anything to the debate, and it presupposes an absurd response. Is there really a white student who is going to say: "I totally disagree.

As a person born without color, I find racism to be loads of fun"? If the information that is provided after the phrase "As a person of color..." *does* relate to the experience of being a person of color, this does not necessarily improve things. Rather than contributing to the "robust exchange of ideas," fronting a statement with an identity tag like *person of color* actually shuts down any exchange of ideas before it begins. Among other things, the mood it induces is one that suggests that anyone who disagrees with or cares to counter the statement is somehow against people of color, and is therefore a racist. The ones who fare the worst are the other persons of color in the classroom, especially ones from the same ethnic group as the original commentator, who might disagree or hold a different point of view. They risk appearing as "sell outs" (that is, minorities who cooperate or agree with the views of the majority group) in front of their peers. Rather than the robust exchange of ideas, we all too often end up with bouts of "identity bullying"—white students are told they "don't understand" and students of color believe they have a viewpoint that cannot be questioned by others. When that happens, it's not diversity. It's just sad.

So what actually happens? What usually happens after these awkward and stilted moments in the classroom is that either my email inbox or my office hours fill up with wonderfully insightful responses from very frustrated students, who add a comment to the effect of "I wanted to say this in class but I was afraid of being called a racist/sell-out/etc." (and not just white students says—students of color say this, too). What is worse, the students who make comments beginning with "As a student of color..." misinterpret the silence that follows as a form of empowerment or an affirmation of their point of view. When diversity emerged as a mode of discourse over two decades ago, one of the claims that was often made was that classrooms were dominated by majority (white) students, and persons of color were afraid to speak out or not allowed to. Diversity policies and programs were supposed to change that, but instead,

Understanding the Misunderstanding

in the flawed and distorted version of diversity we have today, we have merely substituted one silence for another. We're just as ignorant as we were, but now we are ignorant in more diverse ways.

The remnants of the broken dialog on diversity thus persist but in the form of separate conversations in separate rooms. These are the proverbial "safe spaces" that universities are rushing to create on campuses around the country. These safe spaces consist of identity-based spaces where persons from the same group talk among themselves, rather than with people from other groups. I will have more to say on this later in this book, but for now, do take note of the sad irony: the isolated dialogs on diversity that take place in these isolated rooms are discussions of like-minded people from the same group, which means that most discussions of diversity take place among decidedly non-diverse crowds. The dialog falters in the presence of diversity, and the dialog strengthens in the absence of diversity.[10] The retreat into homogeneity is mistaken for a form of empowerment or "community-building." What safe spaces should really offer is a place where individuals from different groups can feel safe talking to different people, where they can both challenge and be challenged in constructive and creative ways by other people with different perspectives. Instead, safe spaces are areas where we can retreat into our own groups and escape from the responsibilities of diversity.

The "safe space effect" plays out in other ways on college campuses as well. I see traces of it for instance in the actions of so many of my students when new faculty are being recruited at the university. If there is a new faculty position open, students often mobilize, after discussions among themselves in their isolated rooms, separated by their separate identities, and emerge with an energized

---

10 See the following YouTube video in which a student is quickly silenced for suggesting that racism exists in non-white groups as well: https://www.youtube.com/watch?v=A8UTj8lQJhY

advocacy to pressure the department to hire a faculty member from their own group. Chinese students want more Chinese faculty; Latino students want more Latino faculty; African-American students want more African-American faculty, and so on. Seriously, is this the best we can do?

Similarly, if I offer an assignment in one of my courses that is wide open to any topic the student wishes to pursue—something I often do to encourage students to explore creatively any topic they want—rather than diversify their interests the students will immediately choose a topic that is based on their own identity. If I teach a human rights course, the Asian students will write on human rights in Asia; the Muslim students will write about the human rights of Muslims; the Hispanic students will write about Hispanic rights. Each paper becomes an individual safe space, bereft of any substantive diversity. If I try to suggest something different, something that might help students *diversify* their interests, they will politely refuse and admit they know nothing about those other cultures or issues. If I ask a Hispanic student to write a research paper on Korean-American issues, there will be only discomfort from the Hispanic student. Students will confess they don't know those other groups, nor do they seem to want to learn about them. Diversity ends up rewarding and encouraging sameness. And incidentally, this is a fundamental flaw of the whole idea of diversity.

Diversity will fail if we cannot even find a way or a space to talk about it collectively and constructively. What we are supposed to have is a discussion that crosses our identity boundaries and brings us closer together—an integrative conversation where we all learn from and about each other. What we have instead is a perennially unfinished conversation that leaves everyone confused, bitter, and suspicious. Anyone who has studied a foreign language knows the frustration of wanting to say something profound but not having the vocabulary or grammar to articulate it. The debate on diversity is a bit like that. It is like trying to have a discussion in a first-semester Spanish class on the legal complexities of restorative justice in Argentina after decades of authoritarian rule. There might be a lot of great ideas, but what you will actually get is simplistic gibberish and frustration all around. What diversity ought to be doing is helping us become fluent in each other, or fluent in the same language of humanity. What we actually have is an adult conversation phrased in terms of baby talk.

As good as it gets? Diversity in America
One of the things I often hear, especially being in Berkeley, is a continuous litany of complaints about America. Sometimes it is from my students, and sometimes it is from my colleagues. To a certain extent, complaint is a good thing: it tells us where things need improvement. The right to complain is also strongly and rightly protected by the Constitution, as a form of free speech. I also understand and applaud the unbridled idealism that many students bring with them to the university, especially to a place like UC Berkeley. One of the things the university is designed to provide and indeed should provide is a haven of free speech where students can explore their own ideas and learn how to question them and learn how to discern good ideas from emotive opinions. Diversity is supposed to enhance and refine this process by providing a richer environment and a larger menu of ideas and experiences with which to compare one's own, but for many reasons, some of which I have already mentioned and many more of which I will discuss in the pages to come, diversity has either failed entirely to do this, or at least has only revealed a fraction of its true potential. When diversity fails, education fails as well.

As a result of my profession, I have been fortunate to have the opportunity to travel to a wide variety of different places, not as a tourist, but as someone whose goal is to understand the way things work on the ground and in the local environment. This is what is called "research" in my profession. Since I work in a field that deals directly with political systems and legal rights, I am always in a situation where I need to evaluate the performance of different systems of politics and justice. I also focus in my work on identity-based rights as human rights, which means I spend a lot of time evaluating different systems of multicultural politics in different countries around the world. I have always been grateful for these opportunities, perhaps most importantly because of the way they allow me to reevaluate everything I grew up learning in America and about America. Rather than *assume* that American democracy is best, I spend most of time questioning *whether* American democracy is the best. When I spend time in other countries, I experience in abbreviated form what it is like to live there, to face the challenges of everyday life that others who live there must face as well. And I sometimes ask myself whether I would want to live there, and whether it would be a better life than the life I have in America. I have not been to every country in the world, and I have not experienced every different cultural environment either, but I have been to and lived in many of them, and based on what I know and what I have experienced, I can say this: if I were not an American citizen now, I would no doubt be one of the millions of people from other parts of the world trying to become one.

I say this not with a blind sense of national pride, but with a well-seasoned sense of scrutiny. Like so many others, I all too frequently feel I have a reason to complain about many aspects of life and politics in the United States. And there have been times when I see and experience things in other countries and cultures that seemed to me to be a better way to do things than what we have in America. But there is a difference between appreciating one or two specific things and appreciating the entire system, even with all of its flaws and shortcomings. And there is a similarly significant difference between complaint as constructive criticism and complaint as uninformed whining. Diversity in America is supposed to expose us to a number of alternative viewpoints and different perspectives in order to give us a more informed choice as to the best way of doing things, not simply for ourselves, but for others as well. Diversity in America is supposed to make us better Americans, and it is supposed to make America the best place it can be. So why has diversity not done this? Why does diversity divide more than it unites, wound more than it heals, scream more than it speaks, irritate more than it elevates?

One of the wonderful things that diversity can do is to provide the same opportunities to experience the different ways of being and different ways of seeing that the world has to offer without ever having to leave the place where you already are. Many people, and in these economic times no doubt most people, cannot afford to travel to other places and other countries and stay there long enough to immerse themselves in a different way of life. Diversity is thus, in a sense, a journey of the mind and spirit. That journey is important enough for us that the government spends enormous amounts of time and resources to engineer public policy designed to provide citizens with a diverse environment, not only in classrooms but also in nearly every venue of public life. It is clear that the policy side of things has not done the most effective job with providing a meaningful and constructive experience of diversity, for reasons I have already mentioned and for other reasons I will discuss in more detail throughout the rest of this book. But diversity is more than just policy; it is part public policy, to be sure, but it is also part *civic responsibility*. This is a key point. That means there is only so much we can expect from the policy side of things, and only so much we can complain about when that policy does not live up to its promise. The rest of our attention should be focused on ourselves, on whether we contributed what we can and how we can to the process of diversity, and whether we have taken advantage as best we can of the opportunities provided to us by this thing called diversity. Diversity is, or at least it should be, a process that is designed to help us find the optimal way to situate ourselves among others. That it has failed to do so is abysmally clear.

More tales of diversity
I will illustrate these ideas through a series of snapshots from moments of encounter I have had with diversity in America. I will start with something simple: the tendency to mistake what is familiar with what is correct. Not long ago I had a French exchange student in one of my courses, newly arrived from France for her first semester at UC Berkeley. She came to my office hours, and after a few minutes of chatting I asked her what she thought of her time in America so far. Her response was that America was a very rude country, unlike what she felt was the warmth and kindness she remembered in France. I asked her why she thought this and her primary example was the way that waiters would bring the bill to your table before you had finished your entire meal. She interpreted the American practice as a rude gesture to tell customers to get out quickly, even while they were still eating. This rudeness, she said, would never be tolerated in France, especially since, as she pointed out, eating was important in French culture (is there a culture where eating isn't important?). If we break down the thought process used to reach her conclusion, it goes something like this: in France we do things a certain way, and I am familiar with that way and therefore understand the reasons behind it, whereas in America things are done in a different and unfamiliar way, so the American way must be the wrong way. By mistaking her own familiar ways with the right or better ways, she reached an untenable conclusion.

For my part, I do not understand why she would not have simply asked why things are done this way in America, rather than reach a conclusion based upon an imperfect and erroneous assumption. That seems to me to be something of a civic, if not also a civil, responsibility. Nevertheless, I proceeded to explain to my student why Americans sometimes bring the bill to your table before you are finished eating: not as an act of rudeness, but as an act of courtesy. If you pay close attention, I explained, you will notice that the waiter or waitress will usually deliver your bill with a statement like "no hurries, whenever you are ready." The courtesy comes from the fact that whenever I decide my meal is finished, I already have my bill and can pay when I am ready to leave without delay. It is an act of courtesy that respects me by valuing my time. What my student also did not know is that I had lived in France previously, some years before. I explained to her how frustrating it was in France to finish a meal and then, after several eternities had passed, have to leave my table and friends to go in search of a waiter, especially in Paris, where the waiters often seemed annoyed that they had to stop the nothing they were doing in order to do the something I had requested. And *that* was the moment when everything changed. Once the American system was explained to her, though she did not have to agree with it, she could at least understand it and more importantly understand why leaving the bill was not a rude gesture. And at the same time, to hear a different perspective on her beloved and familiar French system, from someone outside that cultural frame of reference, that interpreted the experience of dining out in France not as a warm and fuzzy cultural moment but rather a frustrating and annoying one, suddenly let her know that there might be more than one way to see things.

    Admittedly, this is a somewhat simple example. Clearly in other situations, things can become much more complex and much more sensitive and challenging to negotiate. Not long ago I attended an event in Silicon Valley that was designed to celebrate and bring together South Asian entrepreneurs from the high-tech industry for which the area is famous. After the keynote speech, on the topic of culture, there was the usual time for questions from the audience. The first question that was asked was from someone from

India, who, as he explained in his question, had been in America long enough to have had children who were born in America and to raise them in America. His question was this: how can we teach our children to appreciate the good values of India, and how can we protect them from the bad values of America? When the keynote speaker, who was also from India, countered by pointing out that if his children were born in America then they were in fact American and should embrace American values, the person asking the question became flustered, and offered the following observation. India, he said, is like our mother, while America is like our wife. You can always divorce your wife, but you can never abandon your mother. This comment was greeted with applause by some from the audience, but others were visibly uncomfortable with the analogy.

For me, there were a number of things that troubled me about the question and about the analogy. For starters, the suggestion that you could "never abandon your mother" struck me as odd. As someone who has lived in India previously, I remember hearing and reading all sorts of reports of elderly persons—usually mothers—being intentionally abandoned by their families at large religious festivals (such as the Kumbha Mela festival) because their families no longer wanted to care for them. So clearly, it *is* possible to abandon one's mother, even in India. But the analogy itself implied something more troubling for the interwoven social fabric of American life: it implied that wherever one was from originally, that was one's true identity, one's mother identity, and more importantly, that one's mother identity could not and should not be abandoned. I thought immediately of one of the uglier chapters of American history, which was the internment of Japanese-Americans during World War II, something that was sadly done precisely with this type of reasoning in mind: no matter how many generations the Japanese-Americans may have been in America, the reasoning went, they were inescapably and unchangeably

"Japanese." And since Japan was "the enemy," so too were "the Japanese." President Reagan offered an apology and compensation for surviving victims of internment in 1988, and it was made clear then, and in many ceremonies ever since, that this action and the type of reasoning that justified it should never again be repeated in the United States. Yet here was someone in present-day California using the same reasoning—claiming that anyone with roots in India, even if born in America, was inescapably and unchangeably Indian.

It may seem as if the discussion has drifted away from diversity at this point, but in fact it has not. For reasons that I will discuss later in this book, there are many people who believe that maintaining and even celebrating the link to one's country of origin or one's heritage, in this case India, is in fact the best way of participating in diversity in America. Indeed, as some would have it, refusing to let go of one's country or culture of origin is an act of resistance against assimilation to the dominant culture in America, a resistance that supposedly strengthens diversity. But this is not the only way to view this. To return to the original analogy that was offered, of viewing one's country of origin as one's own mother, what if we switch our perspective and see it another way? What if instead of referring to India as mother and America as wife, what if we see India as an arranged or forced marriage (since no one has a choice in the matter of citizenship when they are born), and America as a marriage of choice, or what is called in India a "love marriage"? India was the marriage arranged for you, but America was the one where you truly fell in love.

Suddenly things appear very different. Arranged marriages are still common in India, though this is rapidly changing, and while families often put considerable effort and sometimes coercion into keeping arranged marriages together, sometimes the strain is just too much and they just do not work out. If we apply that to our current example, if someone living in India is looking for opportunities that either do not exist in India or else do exist but due to corruption or discrimination they cannot be obtained, then clearly something is not "working out" in that arrangement. By choice, that person comes to America, where those opportunities do exist and are obtainable. The arranged marriage with India is broken and the love marriage with America begins. The person in question is now in a love marriage with America, or at least with California, in the case of Silicon Valley. Yet suppose also that at every chance and every extended holiday, the man takes his children, even those born of his new "wife" (America), back to his previous "family" (India), and when the new wife finally asks why he does this, he says: "I want to make sure they have the good values of my previous family, and I want to protect them from the bad values you have." Really, in what world would this make sense? In what world would that be acceptable? Nor do I think anyone would disagree with the new wife if she took her husband and kicked him out of the house, or at least made him sleep on the couch until he wised up and figured out what he did wrong. Good diversity, like any good marriage, requires commitment.

Of course, my altered version of the original analogy is not the definitive one, and I am only offering it because I think it's fun to consider. And that is precisely what diversity is supposed to provide: alternative ways of seeing the same situation, to give us new and better ways of seeing our own actions and those of others. The analogies I just discussed, both the original one and my revised version, speak to a central issue in the world of diversity, namely the contribution that more recent and current immigrants make in expanding and enhancing the experience of diversity in America. It is no coincidence that debates on diversity policy often end up morphing into debates on immigration policy. The two are linked but they are not necessarily the same—not every issue involving immigration is also an issue involving diversity policy (there are issues of national security, for instance). The most important area where they are linked is in the discussion of what might be called *civic demeanor*: the positioning of the self in relation to the rest of public society. Many diversity advocates try to argue that the more immigrants we have in America, the better it is for America, that somehow we always and automatically benefit from more and more diversity and difference. But that difference has to be accessible by public society if any benefit is to be derived from it. That is why recent concerns over the growth of ethnic enclaves, particularly in urban areas, generate such concern, since enclaves tend to turn increasingly inward as they grow, making them increasingly inaccessible to outsiders (and hence insulating them from public society). Diversity will never be able to do the work it is supposed to do if the landscape of America becomes divided by ethnic geographies that require shibboleths to get from one part to the next.

Searching for clarity in America
Clarity is the key quality needed here: diversity and immigration are not the same issues, and while it is good to understand how they link together, to confuse them is to diminish the significance of both. Immigration reform is often seen as a battle between those who support the ideas and policies of diversity and those who do not. But there are often two, very different arguments at work here. Take, for instance, the very contentious rhetoric that emerges in any discussion of the legal aspects of immigration in America, and here I'm not even talking about the cantankerous debate about using the word "undocumented" rather than "illegal." No, the debate I'm talking about is the debate on whether opposition to immigration is inherently and necessarily an expression of racism. It can be, of course, but the more general discussion is a really a debate about civic demeanor, and not a debate about race. One side of the debate is arguing that our best civic virtue is *compassion*: should we not be a caring nation that shows compassion to those who have come to this country, sometimes risking great hardship and even

their lives, in the hope of escaping an unbearable life elsewhere and finding a meaningful life here in America? The other side of the debate is arguing that our best civic virtue is *fairness*: should we not be a just nation that shows fairness to all in the enforcement of our laws and the exercise of our ethics? In the latter case, allowing immigrants into the country who arrived through illegal means and offering amnesties to those who entered illegally is in essence unfair to those who have taken the ethical step, often at great risk and hardship, to enter the country and obtain citizenship through legal means. Amnesties, by this argument, make a mockery of fairness and create incentives to undermine the rule of law that is one of the central mainstays of American democracy. Neither side of this debate is focusing on race, and yet, there are individuals and groups who insist on merging these debates with already heated debates on diversity, and the result is that we end up with a simplified and untenable argument that shifts the question from one of citizenship to one of race: either you support the decision to allow all immigrants into the country, regardless of how they entered the country, or you are a racist.[11] When the issues of diversity and immigration get confused, the rhetoric gets contorted, and when the rhetoric gets contorted, the discussion gets convoluted, and when the discussion gets convoluted, the conversation turns to silence, and when the conversation turns to silence, we get nothing.

Another debate that often gets confused and muddled as a debate on diversity is the issue of the status of the English language in America. Should America be an English-speaking nation, or should it recognize "current realities" and accept the inevitable shift to a multilingual country? Here again, simplification and

---

11 For a discussion by Barack Obama on this very claim, see Ben Kamisar, "Obama: Someone opposed to immigration system isn't 'automatically racist'," *The Hill* (April 24, 2017) at http://thehill.com/homenews/news/330239-obama-someone-opposed-to-immigration-system-isnt-automatically-a-racist

distortion are our worst enemies. For one thing, not all advocates of an English-speaking America are necessarily supporters of an "English only" agenda: some are, but most advocate the idea that all Americans should possess the ability to communicate with each other clearly and fluently, regardless of racial or ethnic background. And while supporters of an English-speaking America are often characterized as racists by those who argue that a multilingual America is a more diverse America (and hence those supporting the English language are by definition opponents of diversity), it is far more productive to interpret the support for a common-denominator English language throughout America as a vote *in favor* of diversity, not against it. Think, for instance, of the Supreme Court ruling in the *Grutter* case, discussed previously. Even the majority opinion made it clear that the endpoint of all of these diversity policies and programs that we now have, an endpoint America is supposed to reach within twenty-five years, is *an integrated and inclusive society*, something not possible without a common language. Similarly, it would be nearly impossible to have the "robust exchange of ideas" in our classrooms, something that the Supreme Court felt was the central point of diversity-based policies and programs in educational institutions, if we cannot speak the same language.

Promoting English as a mandatory *common* language is not the same thing as promoting English as the *only* language in America, which is about as misguided and myopic an idea as changing the name of Los Gatos, California, to The Cats. It makes no sense, and it makes no contribution to anything, to confuse the two. The study of foreign languages, as the quote from Goethe I discussed earlier points out, is actually one of the most powerful vehicles we have to expose ourselves to the ways in which others experience the world and the different ways they have of expressing that experience. Just as a finely-tuned approach to diversity in our classrooms and workspaces allows us to travel in our minds to experience different perspectives without ever having to leave our schools and offices, so too does the study of a foreign language afford us the same opportunity for reflection about who we are in relation to others and to see the world anew from another perspective. And yet here, too, the arduous project of diversity comes up short, and less by intrinsic design than by the actions of individuals. I will discuss the consequences of this in more details later in this book, but for now, here is a short version of how this occurs.

Why diversity requires us to be different
If diversity is supposed to afford us the opportunity to experience different ways of seeing, thinking, and experiencing, then it follows that for us to get the most out of diversity we need to explore things that are truly different. Yet in my experience in the world of education, most students will not take advantage of opportunities provided by diversity programs, and will instead choose opportunities that do the opposite. If they study a foreign language, for instance, most students will choose a language that is already familiar to them. Korean-American students will choose to study Korean, Chinese-American students will study Mandarin, Peruvian-American students will study Spanish, and so on. Similarly, in many of the Education Abroad Programs offered by universities around the country, students will often choose to study in countries that are closest to their ethnic background. Korean-American students will go to Korea, Chinese-American students will go to China, Mexican-American students will go to Mexico (or to a nearby Spanish-speaking country), and will hence bypass most of the opportunities and challenges that diversity is supposed to provide. I have occasionally taught in an international summer program in South Korea and am always surprised and quite frankly disappointed by the high percentage—roughly 90%—of students who are Korean-Americans. Given the opportunity to go anywhere in the world for a summer, their first thought is to

choose sameness rather than difference. In essence, they use the opportunities provided by diversity to avoid diversity. This seems to me to be a strong candidate for the "unclear on the concept" award for diversity.

Making a poor choice when provided with the opportunities that diversity should provide is one thing, but to return to my original point at the start of this section about the litany of complaints I hear about America, making uninformed judgments about America due to one's own shortsighted and narcissistic choices is to mobilize ignorance in the service of diversity. So many of the complaints I hear about why the United States is "so messed up" are uninformed assessments based on the fact that the person making the complaint has either (1) not experienced the adversity and the challenges of a different place or (2) the different places they go to are chosen by their ethnic or racial identity, to minimize the degree of difference experienced. As one of my Korean-American students once told me when I asked how her summer in Korea was: Korea was better than America because, as she put it, "It was *soooooo* nice to be somewhere where everyone looked just like me." If diversity has failed to provide so many of the opportunities it was designed to offer, it is partly because of poorly-designed policies, but it is also partly because so many people have failed diversity itself. Better policies can only go so far to make a more diverse America a vibrant, unified, and integrated reality; the rest of the way depends on the quality of the choices we ourselves make, among others.

Goethe was right about languages—we never really understand our own until we learn to speak the language of others. The same lesson is true of diversity, though diversity is more than just being able to talk the talk. More importantly, it asks us to walk the walk. In that sense, both in the talking and in the walking, we have not done the best job we can do in reimagining ourselves among others. Diversity is about learning to walk in someone else's shoes, not about relishing the comfort of our own.

CHAPTER 3

AMERICA: THE IMPROBABLE COUNTRY

America is the most improbable country in the world. If we could somehow get in touch with Bill and Ted and hitch a ride in their most excellent time machine (if you don't get that reference, then by all means ask someone cooler than you), and have them take us to a moment in time before 1776 and to a country outside of America—I will suggest Britain so that Bill and Ted can be closer to their princesses—we would have some very interesting conversations when we talked with political philosophers of the time. If we could sit down at the table with them, and we suggested the idea of a place like America, they would say that the idea was patently absurd, no doubt bound utterly to fail. To think of a country, unknown in its geography and in its landscape, where people would go, with nothing more than what they could carry onto a ship, and after arrival discover (and unfortunately brutalize) a series of other cultures already present in that country but totally foreign to them, and then set up a government that had never really been tried before, go to war with the colonial power that ruled them and then open the country up so that all sorts of new people could flood in: well, no one in their right mind would think any of that would be possible, or perhaps even desirable. Yet America in the present is such a huge part of the world—a familiar presence that is alternatively praised and despised—that it is easy to forget just how radical the whole idea of America was in its origins. The fact that it worked at all, and still works (reasonably) well to this day, is one of the miracles of the modern world.

As if the origins of America were not radical enough, think of the current state of the population in America. Aside from being historically populated by people from every continent on earth, every year the United States takes in more and more new people, from more and more different places, than any other country in the world, at least in terms of sheer numbers. Some of them come in search of a better life, and some of them come to flee the horrors of their native lands (the United States resettles more refugees than any other country in the world), and yet the whole system somehow holds together.[12] To be sure, there have been many problems all along the way, some of them severe, but it again speaks to the strength and well-crafted design of the American system that even in times of crisis, the system has remained sound and sturdy and has weathered crises that have brought other countries and civilizations to a swift and decisive collapse.

America as a nation was hammered out of a thousand forges and mapped out of a thousand pathways. Actually it is probably more than a thousand on both accounts but I was just going for good dramatic effect, mostly to make a point. It is the only country I know of which has its own dream: the American Dream is as well known outside of American as it is inside. On top of that, *diversity* has been a part of America since America was a part of the world, as an idea and then as a reality, and the struggle with the ever-expanding awareness of difference among Americans by Americans

---

12 For refugee resettlement figures, see for instance these facts and figures from the United Nations Refugee Agency: http://www.unhcr.org/52693bd09.html

is a central chapter of the long narrative that makes up American history. That narrative, and that encounter with difference—with the continuously revolving door of newcomers and foreigners and wanderers and immigrants who have made America what it is—has admittedly not always gone well. Sometimes it has gone badly, and sometimes it has gone very badly. But sometimes it has gone very well, even inspirationally so. In any one year, America takes in more people from more diverse backgrounds than many countries have taken in during their entire existence. Yet somewhere and somehow, through all of good and bad times, the idea and promise of America has persevered.

So, if diversity has been a continuous thread in the ongoing story of America's historical development, why then is it such a contentious issue now? Why do our courts clog with case after case of contentious disputes driven by arguments over the perceived fairness or lack thereof regarding identity and diversity? Do we really live at an exceptional moment in American history, when diversity has reached a critical point where if it is not resolved now it will unravel the richly woven cloth of American society? While rumors of any apocalyptic identity conflict in American can be dismissed as something generated more by sensationalism than sense, there does seem to be something troubling about how a concept that is supposed bring us closer together through better understanding has created so much division in the process, based partly on conceptual difference, but based mostly on the more central issue of identity itself. That fissiparous division, and the sense that it is growing wider and deeper with each passing day, should both be considered as the serious wake-up calls that they are. Every generation in American history has had to confront and work through the unresolved baggage they inherit from the previous generation, and for many reasons, diversity has become our issue to resolve in our time. Whether we experience a reawakening or a rude awakening as a nation depends upon whether we get diversity right. Right now, the only thing that is certain is that it all needs to be fixed, and quickly.

The short answer as to how things have gone off course now, and how diversity needs to change with the new circumstances, is this (the longer version will of course follow later): the version of diversity that we have in front of us is different from the diversity of previous generations. It is different insofar as the diversity of our time is not about understanding or marveling at all the different groups in the proverbial American melting pot, as it may have been in the past. Rather, it has now become focused on rendering justice for the perceived injustices that emerged out of identity-based mistreatment in America's past and present. The melting pot, it seems, did not melt all of the groups in America equally: some were left out entirely, while others were burned. The diversity that we now have, a diversity that was forged in the political transformations of the civil rights movement in the 1960s, is based upon obtaining remedy for a long list of historical injustices. And the most effective way to obtain the benefits of diversity policy in the present, at least with the version of diversity we now have, is to document all of the injustices of America, past and present, and then situate oneself, or more accurately, one's identity group, as a victim of that injustice. American history became reshaped, chapter by chapter, as a litany of mistakes and injustices, a project that slowly came to see the values that the country had scripted previously into its history transformed into a cynical tale of so much self-serving hypocrisy by the criminal elites of America.

I have nothing but sympathy for the effort to create a democracy that better serves and gives voice to *all* the people of America rather than just some. But it is difficult at times to discern the subtle difference between fighting for greater inclusion in a society whose demography is reinvented anew every generation, and fighting for revenge against those who are putatively responsible for the long and ever-expanding list of injustices that are continuously unearthed in the cacophonous struggle to design and define contemporary diversity policy. *Diversity has become an act of vengeance, rather than a process of justice.* And if that is what it has become, then it will only and inevitably end in failure.

Freedom and diversity
Setting aside for now the question of what it means to be a victim of history, there is one major aspect of the entire enterprise of diversity that is often overlooked by supporters and detractors alike. In the midst of the rush to inscribe the abuses and injustices that occurred or still persist in America's complex history, no one bothered to notice the extraordinary and nearly unprecedented level of freedom that made this alternative version of history possible. America is one of the very few countries in the world with the openness and willingness to revisit its own past, to reopen old and even forgotten wounds, and strive to make amends for the mistakes that were made. While more extreme proponents of diversity often revile the United States for the many mistakes of its past, there is a more-than-subtle hint of false comparison at work here, especially when America is compared to other countries on the topic of diversity. The reason we do not hear so much about the racism and injustices of other countries in the world is not because they do not have these nefarious sorts of things, but rather because most of these countries practice heavy forms of nationalistic censorship. In most places, anyone who attempts to write about the less-than-perfect reality underneath the official image faces severe and sometimes lethal consequences. In America, anyone who wants to write about their perceived lack of freedom is free to write about their lack of freedom.

Nevertheless, this is no moment to bask in democratic triumphalism. There *are* bleak moments in American history and these do need to be and should be acknowledged. It is a central part of democratic practice to have access to the information of the past and present and to write it out according to one's own interpretive lens. No matter how painful it might be, it needs to be done. If anything has come out of the acrimony of diversity so far, it is that we do indeed have a better-informed and clearer history of who we are as Americans than we did before. In my father's house, for example, there sits a book, no doubt procured during some antique store outing, that is a history textbook once used in American schools just over a century ago. In that book, meant for grade school students, the reader is informed that there are three races in the world: the Whites, the Coloreds, and the Orientals. Not surprisingly, the Whites are singled out as the most civilized of the races. One cringes to read these things now, rightfully so, and the fact that we can read that now and cringe speaks to a better awareness of how people are different from one another and what that difference means (or doesn't mean). We can decry the fact that the book is racist and once inculcated racist values to students, but the fact that we can decry it now is in its own way a positive thing.

Yet while many cringe-worthy elements have been progressively expunged from the textbooks of American history, others have been newly acquired. The idea that the world consists of only three races, with one better than the other two, seems laughably simplistic, but so too does the current caricature that we have of American history, offered up by self-styled radical historians, that can be distilled down to one dose of simplified gibberish: America, some claim, is a country of and for "privileged white men," and everything outside of that, anything that is not white and not privileged is, in a word, *diversity*. Much of this book will be devoted to showing just how far off the mark that assessment is—equally as cringe-worthy as the three-race model of the world—but for now, let me offer an intellectual appetizer in the form of two spin-offs of this simplified perspective that I encounter almost on a daily basis in my professional life.

Sending a wake-up call to the American Dream
The first one is articulated in the form of a cynical cliché: "The American Dream is a myth." The idea here is that either the American Dream is some kind of emotional opiate to induce Americans to dream that America is good in spite of the harsh reality that surrounds them, or else that it is the dream only of white privileged men and for everyone else it is a nightmare, or more simply, a myth. I do not really need to debunk this so much as confess that I have never understood why this is a problem or even considered a thought-provoking observation. The difference between a dream and a myth is not all that significant anyway. If I have a wonderful dream—there is a reason we wish someone "sweet dreams" before they sleep—it leaves me with a good feeling, though I know it is only a dream. And if the American Dream is a myth rather than a dream, well, what culture doesn't have myths? And what do myths do? They are usually well-crafted stories designed to inculcate positive values, so I am not sure where the harm lies in that either. There is a dream or a myth that tells me I can be anything I want and can choose from an endless menu of things. Is this really some kind of awful thing? Some sort of perverted conspiracy? Yet somewhere along the way, through the warped vision of our current practice of diversity, the idea that the dream became a myth was meant to convey the idea that America tells you that you can be anything you want but in reality, you cannot. So, the great insight of radical history is that dreams and reality are not the same? Gee, I'm floored.

There is no great conspiracy here, and the idea that only some people, perhaps privileged white men, get to be what they want and everyone else has to eat their rancid leftovers does not hold up well under even minimal scrutiny. The essential point of the American dream is that you have the freedom to dream, not that all of your dreams will come true. If I dream I want to be president one day, and it never happens, I have not been wronged by the United States, and the American Dream has not failed me. What the American Dream suggests is that the road to other possibilities and other lives wanders far longer here in America than it does anywhere else. And on that road I have the right to dream as much as I have the right to fail and to make mistakes and to start all over again. I can even pull off that road, sit down, and drink enough beer to puke in the desert while I stare at the stars and sing Pink Floyd songs out of key. I am sure somewhere in America, that is someone's dream, and somewhere else in America, someone's peculiar reality. The point is, all the American Dream says is that you live in a wide-open country that lets you dream of something better than what you have. What it does not say is that if you dream of something better and it does not happen, the government owes you a refund. Maybe the dream is a myth or the myth is a dream, but it seems quite harmless, and I am not sure why this has become the cynical mantra of the critics of diversity.

The second spin-off is like the set up for a call-and-repeat joke, as when a comic will start a joke with something like "Last night it was sooooo cold..." and the audience will shout back "How cold was it?" There are many commentators on diversity in America who love to start a discussion about America with the introductory phrase, "America is sooooo racist..." And after we shout back, "How racist is it?" the answers occur in a number of stock responses. I hear these stock responses all the time, and so I can repeat them like they are folktales. Here are two of the most common standard responses that I hear.

Standard Response #1: *America is so racist because if you look different they will ask you where you are from.*

In other words, they will make the assumption that you are not or could not be American. The first question we have here is who "they" are when "they" make these assumptions and ask these questions. Although the assumed answer will be that "they" are white people, based on my personal observations I can assure you that all sorts of different people—a very diverse crowd—ask these questions. I have seen Asians struggle with the question of whether a Spanish-speaking person is American, South American, Latin America, Latino, or Hispanic. I have seen Latinos struggle with the question of whether an Asian person is Asian or Asian-American. There is no special "knowledge of color" that exempts non-white persons from this line of inquiry. So if it is racist to ask someone where they are from, then it speaks to the diversity of racism that I mentioned in the introduction to this book, because I have seen people from pretty much every different identity group do this.

From a different perspective, however, we could also see the question as a polite one. Why is it preferable to assume that everyone we meet in America is American? I have met plenty of students and know plenty of people who were born in foreign countries and still hold their original (non-American) citizenship, but nevertheless grew up in America with other members of their family who live in America. When they speak, they speak an English that is readily identifiable as an American accent—you wouldn't know they weren't American—but they are in fact not American, at least not by citizenship. I myself have even made the mistake on some occasions of meeting persons from Canada and assuming that they were Americans. Being Canadians, they are usually quite polite about the error, and suspect no malice and take no offense, although once or twice some have reacted with outrage, which in Canadian terms means they smiled with slightly less enthusiasm.

I can offer a more specific example of this rather common argument, one that I have heard consistently for many years: this is the claim that America is racist because when Americans see someone who looks Asian, they will ask the unacceptable question:

Are you Asian? Again, the idea is that asking someone if they are Asian implies that Asians cannot possibly be Americans because they just don't *look* American. (This is the "perpetual foreigner" argument that many Asian-American activists often and erroneously use to show that America is inherently racist.) In this scenario, of course, the person who is put into the role of hypothetical questioner is the average white American, though we have no evidence that whites do this any more or any less than any other identity group. I would suggest that there is a different way to see this, one that will lead us to a different root cause that transforms this from a *one-group-offends-another-no-matter-what-they-do* situation to a *both-sides-need-to-do-a-better-job-of-figuring-out-who-they-are* scenario. To do this, we will need to borrow Bill and Ted's time machine one more time, but only for a short trip, and this time we can stay in America.

On December 16, 2000, actress Lucy Liu hosted the long-running and wonderfully creative sketch-comedy show Saturday Night Live. During her opening monologue, Lucy Liu made the claim—which is true—that she was the first *Asian woman* to host the show. The first Asian host of Saturday night live was Jackie Chan, who is in fact from Asia and also not a woman, but the important thing here is that Lucy Liu is Asian-*American*. Yet she chose to identify herself as Asian rather Asian-American. Does this mean she was racist toward herself? Obviously not, but what it does show more importantly is that there is considerable slippage between the terms Asian and Asian-American. "Asian" is used to describe someone from Asia, as with Jackie Chan, but it is also used, even by Asian-Americans, as a way of describing a general ethnic category. The key issue here might be the slippage between the terms, something common even in the Asian-American community, so it would be premature to jump to the conclusion that anyone who asks an Asian-looking person in America if they are Asian is somehow being racist. It could be a general query, as in, what *kind* of Asian the person is: Chinese? Japanese? Korean? And each of those have the same slippage problems: to be Korean could mean someone from Korea, or an American of Korean descent. Even Korean-Americans often drop the "-American" part of the phrase—Korean-American students tell me all the time that they are *Korean*—so the confusion is not just that of other Americans, but also of Americans of Asian descent who use both labels almost interchangeably. That does not make Americans racist, it just makes them confused.

Around the same time that Lucy Liu was hosting Saturday Night Live, I was asked to be the faculty moderator of an event at UC Berkeley hosted by the Asian Student Association (ASA) completely devoted to the rather puzzling question: "Are Filipinos Asian?" Keep in mind that the Asian Student Association, a group composed of students who call themselves Asian, consists primarily of Asian-American students. But the question of the night was quite intriguing, and so I began my hosting duties that evening by posing a question to all those in attendance, namely, How many people here think that Filipinos are *not* Asian? The response was quite interesting: by a show of hands, it was clear that all the Filipinos present considered themselves to be Asian, but the vast majority of the other Asians (including Asian-Americans) did not. When I asked the non-Filipino Asians why they thought Filipinos were not Asian, the most common answer was also the simplest: they were "too different" to be Asian. Among other responses I heard were these: that Tagalog was not really an Asian language, that most Filipinos were Catholic which was "not an Asian religion," and that there was too much Spanish and American influence for them to be truly Asian. Quite frankly, I found all of these answers decidedly absurd—it is up for the Filipinos to decide who and what they are—but for the moment, consider the interesting parallel. If Americans are racist because they cannot see Asians as Americans, and if they cannot do that because Asians are "too different," weren't these Asians equally racist for claiming Filipinos cannot be Asian because they are also too different? As I said in the introduction, once we move past the simplicity of our current diversity discourse, it is easy for anyone to see that racism in America is as diverse as America itself.

If that example isn't quite clear enough, we can jump-cut to another moment in time in the world of popular culture. In 1991, director Mira Nair's film *Mississippi Masala* was released in the United States. The film depicts the difficult relationship between an African-American man named Demetrius (played by Denzel Washington), and an Indian woman named Mina (played by Sarita Choudhury), whose family has relocated to the United States from Uganda (which has a sizeable Indian community). The film has much to say about diversity and identity, but for now I would like to focus on two juxtaposed scenes from the film to discern what their differences can tell us about the representation of diversity-related encounters in popular culture. In the first scene, Mina is in the supermarket and is filling her cart with several gallons of milk, when a supermarket clerk, who is white, asks rather doltishly if she is going to open a dairy. Mina shoots him a look of disgust and disdain, and the message is clear: the white employee's ignorance of Indian culture and culinary traditions is interpreted as an act of racism and (white) stupidity. In the second scene, however, Mina and Demetrius are in the car and Mina mentions the term "masala." Demetrius responds with the question: "Is that some sort of religious thing?" Though Demetrius's question reveals the same level of ignorance of Indian culture and culinary traditions as the white supermarket clerk, this time Mina responds with a generous and flirtatious smile and offers a detailed explanation of what masala means (*masala* refers to the blends of spices in Indian cuisine).

It is hard to interpret the glaring differences between these two scenes, and viewed side by side, they raise a number of uncomfortable questions relating to diversity. Two statements of cultural ignorance are presented to the same character (Mina), but one generates disdain and the other generates allure. I suppose we could point out that Denzel Washington's character is attractive and handsome, and the supermarket clerk is, well, not, but that leaves us with the unacceptable conclusion that the level of racism embedded in a statement is in inverse proportion to the attractiveness of the speaker. As long as someone is sexually attractive, then apparently their racism only adds to their charm. But this is hardly a constructive standard to work with. Other observers might suggest that the difference in the scenes comes from different expectations, as in, we expect the white character to be more aware of cultural differences, but for the African-American character, we keep our expectations lower. I think the problem with that approach is self-evident.

So perhaps the answer lies in understanding the actions of each character in a larger context. By this argument, we have to assume, especially since we have no direct evidence in the film itself, that Mina's character has suffered repeated cultural misunderstandings from white people, and that those misunderstandings were all generated by some sort of implicit or explicit racist impulse, whereas she experienced only very few if any such misunderstandings from African-Americans. But that could also be due to the fact that she has had far fewer encounters with African-Americans, making for a skewed and unreliable comparison, or it could be due to the fact that Mina attributes a different motive to white misunderstandings than she does to misunderstandings from other identity groups, making Mina herself the racist. It is unclear why Mina could not have been as affable and amiable with the supermarket clerk as with Demetrius. Had she simply explained to the clerk that the dairy products were going to be used to make home-made paneer or yoghurt, for instance, the supermarket clerk would have learned a new cultural artifact that might have positively transformed the way he interacted with other Indians in the store for the rest of his life, or at least the rest of his career as a supermarket clerk. That would have been a positive example of diversity in action, but it would have also made for a less sensationalist and provocative film.

Standard Response #2: *America is so racist because if you look "different" people will ask you if you speak English and even if you do, they will tell you that your English is very good.*

As with Standard Response #1, "people" in this version are always assumed to be white people, an assumption that is distortively and disturbingly wrong. One can find this Standard Response applied to other "Western" countries as well. When I was in Singapore for a semester as a visiting Fulbright Scholar, one student at my host university made a comment about how Australia was "such a racist country." When I asked why she felt Australia was so racist, she replied that it was because when she went to Australia—she was an ethnic-Chinese Singaporean and in Singapore education is primarily offered in the English language—Australians, by which she meant white Australians, would tell her that she spoke "very good English." I then asked this student to walk over to the window with me, a window that looked out over a busy street in a bustling part of Singapore. For background, I should point out that Singapore's population is around 75-80% ethnic Chinese, so in any given part of Singapore, you are bound to find people who "look Chinese." I asked her to look out at the crowded sidewalk, and to tell me which of the people who "looked Chinese" were from Singapore, and which were not, and which of them spoke English, and which of them didn't. Then I asked her which of them were Chinese-Australian. And of course she could not tell any of those things from merely looking at them—the only thing she could say with any certainty was that they "looked Chinese." Then I asked her what she might say if we went down to the sidewalk and started talking to random people who "looked Chinese," and suppose one of them responded with an unmistakable Australian accent.

Would the student respond with surprise, or with a statement like, "Oh, I didn't know you were from Australia!" and implying that due to her Chinese appearance she did not think or know she was Australian? And if my student did say that, would she also be "so racist"? Suddenly, Australia didn't look so racist after all.

But let us look at the converse to this for a moment. What if no one in America (or Australia) bothered to ask the question and simply assumed that everyone in America whom they encountered was completely fluent in English. When you meet someone on the street, you have no idea who they are: perhaps a tourist from Bolivia, or a recent immigrant from Vietnam, or a refugee from Syria, or someone from Russia here to visit a friend. All of them could look like any other person born in America, but unlike someone born in American, it would be entirely possible that none of them could speak English. So where is the harm in asking, if you are not sure? Besides, if no one asked the question and simply assumed that everyone spoke English, chances are pretty good that Standard Response #2 would then change to *America is so racist because people here assume that everyone in the world speaks English.*

In the San Francisco Bay Area, where I live, I usually make a trip to one or more Asian grocery stores about once every two weeks. Having lived in different parts of Asia, I have developed a taste for a number of Asian dishes that I now consider comfort food, even though I grew up with none of them. I like to make these dishes at home, and so off to the markets I go to get the ingredients. When I am in the Asian grocery stores, the one language that strikes me as decidedly foreign is in fact English. Depending on the shop I am in, I might hear Cantonese, Mandarin, Hokkienese, Vietnamese, Lao, Khmer, Thai, or any one of a number of other dialects. If I hear English, it actually stands out as strange and foreign. More often than not, if I am looking for something and cannot find it, when I ask someone who works at the store, they will make a hand gesture that tells me to wait, because they need to find someone who can speak English. One of the stores I go to in Oakland actually has a sign that says "Our staff speak limited English—Please Be Patient." In any case, if I then switch to the language of the person I just asked—Thai for instance—this will almost immediately be followed by a gesture of surprise and a remark to the effect of "wow, you speak very good Thai." Apparently, because I "didn't look Thai" they assumed I could not speak Thai and when I did they wanted to comment that I spoke it well. Hm, sound familiar?

Now I suppose in that moment I could start foaming at the mouth and decry the fact that the person who said this to me made the assumption that I was not from Thailand, and therefore I was "too different" to be Thai. Or I could just walk away and tell all of my American friends that "Thai people are sooooooo racist." But perhaps I could do something decidedly different: I could strike up a friendly conversation—the way that Mina might have done with the supermarket clerk—and explain how I learned Thai and why I had spent time in Thailand and in the course of the conversation I might have made a new friend and also might have made this person understand that not just Thai people appreciate Thai culture or speak Thai. It is always unclear to me why the civil route to diversity is not the preferred one, and why the first assumption that gets made is one of hostility and spite, and why the first response is an accusation of racism. Unless of course you are talking with Denzel Washington. Apparently, that changes everything: remember, according to Mira Nair, if the person you are talking with is handsome or sexy, then their ignorance and racism should be overlooked.

What I also find enlightening is that I get the exact same reaction whenever I am in Asia, and yet at no point do I assume that racism or hostility is involved. I have spent a considerable amount of my life studying a number of foreign languages, and yet everywhere I go, there is the same reaction of surprise and the same *compliment* that I speak "good" Korean, Thai, Tamil, etc. Many Asians complain that too many foreigners, especially English-speaking ones, assume that everyone in Asia somehow knows English. Even in Singapore, where English is the medium of instruction and one of the official languages of the country, you will sometimes meet shopkeepers, taxi drivers, and many others who cannot communicate effectively in English. If I walk into a Korean bank and want to carry out any type of complex financial transaction—perhaps wire funds from my Korean bank account to my American bank account—I will usually want to verify the request in English. The Korean number system is complex, there are two different sets of numbers (one pure Korean and one Sino-Korean), and large numbers are grouped differently than in the American counting system, so for instance 600,000 is seen as 60 quantities of 10,000. So sometimes I fear that perhaps I misspoke and requested to transfer sixty billion dollars, or some other fantastic sum. Yet when I want to verify the transaction in English, even if I know the bank employee knows English (for instance by overhearing conversations while I wait), I will still ask in Korean if he or she knows English, out of courtesy and respect. Not out of racism—out of courtesy and respect.

To bring this back to America, the fact is that there are many Americans, and many people living in America (but without American citizenship), who do not speak English, or who do not yet feel comfortable speaking English but are learning. It is hard to tell this just by appearance. The rules of civility and courtesy tell us that when we are in doubt, we should ask, so it is always something of a puzzle to me why asking someone if they speak English, particularly if there are any grounds for uncertainty, makes someone a racist. It might equally be an act of courtesy. This is not to deny the possibility that some people do ask the question with a sense of malice or a sense of racism, but it bespeaks of extremely poor judgment to assume that every instance carries the same intent every time. If diversity teaches us to understand difference, it means not just understanding different people and different cultures, but also different contexts and different interactions and different experiences. Just as we cannot assume that all Asian people are the same, we cannot assume that every question has the same intent. Diversity is in many ways the process of disentanglement.

America among others
While it is important to view and evaluate America based on its own standards and principles, there are times when a comparative perspective becomes powerfully revealing, especially insofar as it offers a new way of re-examining what happens in the United States. Among other things, it offers a different way to rephrase the many questions of diversity. The statements above that start with the phrase "America is so racist…" would have to be asked and answered differently if the question were switched to a comparative one: If America is so racist, then what other countries are less racist? Or more racist? If America is so racist, why do so many people keep trying to come here? Few people have credible answers to these questions, and mostly because they either have very little meaningful experience in other countries and contexts, or else their evaluation is based upon a highly flawed and biased sense of comparison drawn largely from the type of myopic vision generated by identity-based narcissism (more on which is below).

For my part, I have spent a considerable amount of time in other countries and in other cultural environments, and I can say that I have never been in any social or cultural environment in any other country where discrimination, if not outright racism, did not exist. What separates the experience in America from what happens elsewhere, based on my experiences and observations abroad, is not that racism and discrimination do not happen here, but rather that (1) there is a strong and prevalent belief that discrimination is wrong and should not happen, and (2) there is far *less* discrimination and violence in relation to the degree of demographic complexity in society. Note that in the latter point, what is *not* being said is that there is no discrimination at all or that because there is less discrimination and racism in America than in other countries, there is cause for celebration or at least no real need for concern. Having seen other countries with very little demographic complexity implode with only the smallest of catalysts, I am always aware how easily things can fall apart. It is disconcerting to think of just how quickly identity-based issues can destroy an entire society.

Leaving America behind for a moment
With that cheery thought in mind, we can make a different sort of perspectival leap—not the chronological one made possible by a fantastical time machine, but a geographic one, made possible by a more familiar machine, the airplane. Suppose we take a trip to, say, South Korea, and have a look around and then stand there and look back at America. And let's take up the complex and challenging issue of refugees and refugee resettlement. As I said earlier, America takes in more refugees from more different ethnic backgrounds than any other country in the world. In 2012, for instance, the United States, with a population of 310 million people, took in nearly 300,000 refugees. South Korea, by contrast, with a population of around 50 million people, or about one-sixth of the United States, took in around 1,700. The majority of refugees in South Korea are refugees from North Korea; South Korea accepts them automatically as refugees due to the fact that they are of the same ethnic background. (Almost all Asian countries show a strong racial preference not only in their acceptance of refugees but also in their granting of citizenship.) Non-Korean refugees must go through an entirely different and more arduous process. South Korea did not sign the Refugee Convention, the central document of international human rights legislation that

forms the basis of refugee law, until 1992, and did not accept its first non-Korean refugee until 2001. The first non-Korean refugee to obtain Korean citizenship did not occur until March of 2010, something that South Korea tried to push as a message to the rest of Asia to do a better (and less racist) job. This is Asia, after all, where refugees are not usually welcome, unless they come from the right racial or ethnic background.

Now, let's compare the South Korean experience with the American experience. If South Korea has one-sixth the population of the United States, then the proportionate share of refugees that it should accept, if it wished to set its refugee policy on par with America, would be one-sixth of the American amount, or 50,000 new refugees per year. With only 1,750 refugees, that ends up being only a small fraction, around 3.5%, of what the United States takes in. Based on my experiences and observations living in South Korea, most South Koreans would have a very hard time accepting 50,000 new non-Korean refugees every year. Even with the small number of refugees and foreigners in South Korea, incidents involving racism and discrimination are alarmingly high. They represent the highest number of complaints to the Korean Human Rights Commission in Seoul. The treatment of foreign "mail-order brides" from Southeast Asia is so appalling that Cambodia recently passed a law forbidding Cambodian women from marrying Korean men (currently the law has been changed to apply only to Korean men over 50 years of age). As of 2011, South Korea had just over 3,000 immigrant children, and of those, only 31% attended formal schools, largely due to the intolerable discrimination they faced among Korean students.[13] South Korea's typical answer is to create alternative places and schools for foreigners, rather than

---

13 These figures are taken from the *Munhwa Ilbo* (July 12, 2011) [in Korean] at http://www.munhwa.com/news/view.html?no=2011071201070527258004

confront and address the deep-seated prejudice that lurks just under the surface of Korea's ethnically homogeneous society.

I have lived in South Korea several times, and have traveled extensively throughout the Korean peninsula, including North Korea. When I am in Seoul, I usually live—my Korean host university makes the housing arrangements—in an apartment complex that is entirely separate from the places where ordinary Koreans live. Indeed, the sign on the front of the building states clearly in English: "Apartments for Foreigners." There is a bus at this facility that takes residents to other locations in the city, and a sign on the front of the bus warns other Koreans, "Foreigners on board," lest they become polluted through contact with non-Korean people. When I teach a course in South Korea, if I look at the student roster I receive at the start of the semester, Korean students are listed by their major, while non-Korean students are merely labeled "Foreigner." In essence, you are either Korean, or you are just a bland, blended non-Korean frappuccino of "everything else" that comes in only one flavor: foreign.

I have had many other personal encounters with Korea's desire to contain the foreigner and limit the foreign presence in Korea. Once, I was walking around Seoul with a female colleague, who was Korean, in a wonderful old neighborhood just to the east of Gwanghwamun. As we strolled down a narrow street, in the midst of art studios and teahouses, a man came running up, clearly agitated, and demanded to know what the woman was doing with me. What was interesting to me was that the man directed all of his questions, and his increased agitation, only toward her: clearly he assumed that as a foreigner, there could be no way I would know a word of Korean (in reference to the earlier discussion of assuming people who look different cannot speak the local language, sound familiar?). What upset him was the possibility that a Korean woman might have an intimate relationship with a non-Korean man (in fact, our relationship was one of professional friendship and nothing more). He demanded to know if we were married, and if not, he told my colleague that it was wrong to be with me. I suppose if we *were* married, she would be a lost cause anyway, at least in the eyes of this Korean man. Korean women who become romantically involved with non-Korean men do tend to be seen negatively, though this is slowly changing. I tried to interject my own comment into the increasingly heated conversation, but the minute I said something in Korean, the man looked at me in the way someone would look at their dog, if their dog suddenly started speaking Korean instead of just barking. Then he ran off.

When I tell the story of this encounter to other Koreans or Korean-Americans, what strikes me most is how they cannot see what is wrong with the encounter, and especially for Korean-Americans, how they cannot see any parallel at all to an encounter like that in America, where it would *clearly* be racist.[14] The most common excuse I hear—and it is an excuse, not an explanation—is that Korea is a very homogeneous society, and therefore has strong cultural values as well as close-knit family groups and strong inter-personal bonds. These close-knit relationships are what make Korean society and culture so strong, it is argued, and therefore it makes sense that outsiders would be seen as a threat. It should not be seen as discrimination, the argument goes, but rather as cultural strength and protection, which somehow makes it all okay. If I bring America into the conversation, of course, everything changes. Since America is multicultural, it therefore and ironically has no culture to protect, and so it is wrong in America to do these things. But it is good in Korea, it is argued, because of its strong culture and homogeneity.

---

14 For more on this, see Alexis K. Barnes, "Why do non-white immigrants face so much racism in South Korea?" *Vice* (June 5, 2014) at https://www.vice.com/en_us/article/nnq3v8/south-koreas-not-so-subtle-racist-hiring-practices-0000313-v21n5

The argument is disturbing and unacceptable on many levels, but the most egregious reason that it offends is in what it says about diversity: if we accept this argument about Korea, then we must also accept that diversity is a liability, not an asset. The lesson it offers to America is that it would be a good thing to choose one culture, for an example let us choose your basic white and Christian culture, and then force everything else to the margins or force it out entirely. Would that make America great again? I am aware that there are many people who think that America is actually like that, but most of those people say so either because they have never been outside of America to experience other places and environments or because they spent most of their childhoods drinking lead-based paint straight from the can. In pretty much any situation I can think of, if you hear someone in America say that the best approach is to save the white people and get all the "foreigners" out, you would of course call them a racist. So why then would we give South Korea a pass? Because it was "smart" enough to keep the foreigners out? Because it was "smart" enough to discriminate against outsiders? If diversity is the asset we are led to believe, the inherently good thing that the Supreme Court advocated in *Grutter*, then it should be an asset everywhere else as well. And when countries like South Korea keep their refugee and immigrant levels so extraordinarily low, especially compared to the United States, we should see it for the discrimination that it is. Seen from a different perspective, the perspective of Korea's inherently racist behavior, for instance, American diversity looks like a new American revolution every single day.

Again, the point is not made in the spirit of nationalistic triumphalism. The point is not to say that the United States takes in more refugees and immigrants than other countries and therefore critics of America should be quiet. But it does say that those critics, whose work is invaluable to the ongoing project of diversity, at least have the responsibility of developing their critiques from a broader, more informed viewpoint. This is, after all—and noted with a certain degree of irony—precisely the type of viewpoint that diversity is supposed to provide us with, one forged from many different perspectives, and so for anyone with an interest in diversity, the work is our own as much as it is someone else's. Even a quick glance at the South Korean "model"—if we can call it that—shows a startling degree of racism for such a low-level of diversity. What surprises about the American version is actually how little racism there is for such an unprecedented degree of social diversity and complexity. What also sets it apart from so many other places is the persistently stubborn belief that this ongoing experiment with diversity can and will work its magic one day, and the uncompromising stand that discrimination and racism are always and everywhere wrong. Quite rare, that. Almost dreamy.

Refugees, migrants, America, and the world
When the refugee/migrant crisis first started in Europe in the summer of 2015, first Europe and then the entire world witnessed heartbreaking and emotionally distressing scenes of suffering and desperation. Millions of people had fled their homes, some in search of a better life, some to escape from the devastation of war in places like Syria, and almost all of them were trying to find a way to get to Europe. The arrival of so many people in Europe didn't just create emotional turmoil and humanitarian sentiment among many in Europe. It also generated a massive tide of political debate within Europe, a tide that moved across the Atlantic Ocean and became a central issue in the US presidential election campaigns in 2016. Some called for open borders, multiculturalism, and a compassionate response. Others called for closing borders, building walls, and protecting national identities. There wasn't a single election in Europe, including the referendum on Brexit, that was left untouched by this tide of political debate.

The migrant/refugee crisis (migrants and refugees have a different legal definition) was in many ways a crisis of diversity as well. Aside from concerns over national security—what if some of these migrants and refugees were really terrorists?—the concerns over national identity were the ones that spoke most directly to the issues we are dealing with here in our discussion of ourselves among others. Was diversity always a good thing? Or was too much diversity a liability, to the point where France was no longer French, or Germany no longer German? As Europe hesitated, tragedy escalated. Perhaps no greater symbol of the tragedy and hardship these refugees and migrants faced was the tragic death of Alan Kurdi, a three-year old Kurdish refugee from Syria who drowned in the Mediterranean in early September 2015. The photograph of his lifeless body on the beach went round the world, leaving anguish and sadness in its wake. In the face of such human tragedy, how could Europe hesitate? How could Europe do anything other than accept all the refugees and offer them shelter, refuge, and a better life? For many, the answer to these questions was clear and simple. Europe didn't want these refugees and migrants because Europeans are racists.

Europe, in other words, is *just so racist*, or just as racist as America, because they are not accepting refugees and migrants, presumably because the refugees and migrants are different and Europeans don't want the difference that diversity brings. But this argument brings to the surface a number of things about diversity that are as relevant to Europe as they are to America. For one, if Europe is such a racist, inhospitable, and intolerant place, then why are so many refugees and migrants risking everything they have, including their lives, to get there? Embedded in the accusation against Europe is the assumption that other non-European places are somehow *not* racist, so why aren't the migrants and refugees going to places like, say, China? Migrants and refugees may be desperate, but they are also intelligent. There is a reason they headed for Europe, and the reason is that Europe was in fact the *least racist choice* of all the other possibilities. We thus end up with a false impression. Europe looks more racist only because it has to deal with migrants and refugees in ways that do not exist in other countries, largely because those other countries have made it clear they won't accept them.

Since I mentioned China, for example, I should point out that China currently hosts about 300,000 refugees, which is still a much, much smaller percentage per capita than the United States or Europe. But look more closely, and you will notice the vast majority of those refugees are from Vietnam, and more importantly, that they are *ethnic Chinese* from Vietnam (the equivalent in Europe would be to accept only white refugees of European descent). Indeed, China has made it clear it has a strong ethnic/racial preference for refugees, migrants, residents, and even naturalized citizens. This is why there are only 30 Syrian refugees in China, and even then, China has made it clear they are only there temporarily and will be sent along elsewhere.[15] They won't be allowed to settle in China. China has tried to make the argument that their stance isn't about race or ethnicity, instead saying the refugee crisis is Europe's fault and so Europe has to pay for and deal with it, but that kind of logic, which isn't accurate anyway, doesn't apply when it comes to humanitarian assistance. If a severely burned person comes to your door and says their house just burned down and they need help, only an insensitive fool says they won't help because they didn't start the fire.

This isn't an isolated case either. In August 2001, the container ship *MV Tampa* rescued what the crew thought was a boat full of refugees adrift in the sea somewhere in between Indonesia and

---

15 For more on this, see Liang Pan, "Why China Isn't Hosting Syrian Refugees," *Foreign Policy* (February 26, 2016) at http://foreignpolicy.com/2016/02/26/china-host-syrian-islam-refugee-crisis-migrant/

Australia. When the captain of the ship radioed to international maritime authorities to request advice, they informed him that he should take the refugees to the nearest safe harbor, which was in Indonesia. When the captain informed the refugees that he was taking them to Indonesia, however, the refugees then turned on the crew and demanded to be taken to Australia. They didn't want to go to the *nearest* place, they wanted to go to the *better* place (at least according to their idea of which place was better). Fearing for the safety of his crew, the captain radioed the Australian authorities to say he was bringing them to Christmas Island, an outlying island far off the coast of Australia but legally part of Australia. Australia initially refused entry to the *Tampa*, on the grounds that Indonesia was the closer destination, but the captain decided the security situation was too serious on board and so ignored the refusal and went directly to Christmas Island.[16] An investigation would subsequently reveal that the refugees, who came mostly from Iraq, Afghanistan, and Sri Lanka, did not want to go to Indonesia because they had actually just left from there. Indonesia had no interest in accepting any of them as refugees or migrants (though they did say they would accept any of them who were Indonesian), and the refugees on the boat had managed to pay smugglers and corrupt officials to be put on a barely-seaworthy boat and left to drift on the current toward Australian waters.

If this were a book on refugee crises, I would take the time to launch a thorough discussion of Australia's migrant/refugee policies in the aftermath of the *Tampa* affair. But our focus here is on diversity, so there is really only one part of Australia's policy and response I want to focus on, and that is Australia's open question of why people were criticizing Australia and *weren't* criticizing

---

16 For a news report of the affair, see Annabel Crabb, "Tampa enters Australian waters with 433 asylum seekers on board," *Australian Broadcasting Corporation* at http://www.abc.net.au/archives/80days/stories/2012/01/19/3412121.htm

Indonesia. This question, which dovetails nicely with the question of why people aren't criticizing China for doing nothing to help Syrian refugees, is what brings us back to diversity. In a later chapter, I will dive into the turbulent waters surrounding the ongoing debate about whether or not only white people can be racist. I mention that here because the answer to the question is in some sense a variation of or spin-off from that debate. The reason you don't hear more voices criticizing Indonesia for its flagrant mistreatment of refugees/migrants, or more voices criticizing China's racial filter on its refugee acceptance policy, is because to do so would be to open the possibility that Indonesian or Chinese people can be racist, and as we will see in the later discussion, there are many people who simply feel that isn't possible. Therefore, countries like Australia, the United States, or pretty much all of Europe bear the criticism for being racist when it comes to migrant/refugee policy, or immigration in general, because those countries are supposedly "white," which in turn is why they can be racist.

But note how this latter point actually ends up entrenching racism by those who claim to be against it. As I mentioned a bit earlier in this chapter, there are many people who complain that America is completely racist because white people assume all non-whites must be from somewhere else or at least aren't "really" American. Proponents of diversity as a visibility project (putting more non-whites in the room) say this is necessary so that white people understand the country is composed of all sorts of different people with all sorts of different cultural backgrounds. This is where things get distressing. Proponents of this sort of diversity argue that we have to dismantle the idea that America is white, yet this means that if we say that America's migrant/refugee/immigration policy is racist, and if we believe that only whites can be racist, then it must also be the case that only white people are truly American. We end up having to assume that non-whites aren't really a part of America because if they were, then they'd be racist, too, which is allegedly impossible. By excluding non-whites from America, proponents of diversity end up entrenching the "perpetual foreigner" problem discussed earlier, rather than dismantling it.

On a final note, let me emphasize that none of this implies that those who criticize the migrant, refugee, or immigration policies of the US, Europe, or Australia are wrong or have no right to make the criticism. My point is to show how debates that emerge out of the language of diversity end up impoverishing the discussions we have about other global issues. And let us not forget those who suffer the most due to this truncated, distorted discussion of what is truly a global crisis, and that would be the refugees themselves.

One America, many, or none at all?
It would be one thing if these ideas about how racist America is and how diversity is somehow the simple and magical antidote to racism were just idle debates among a handful of people in near-empty classrooms or whispered conversations in a bar in the weirdly-shaped corner booth with bad lighting and bad acoustics. But these are not merely the misguided notions of the few; they are words of anti-wisdom carried by non-intuitive trains of twisted logic directly into the heart of our public lives. Here, for instance, is a story of how this type of anti-wisdom is passed on to others.

I once spoke at an event with another faculty member at UC Berkeley for which the topic was this: What advice should we give to graduating Asian-American students as they move on to the next step in their career trajectories? There were only the two of us, just me and the other professor, and we were supposed to speak for fifteen minutes each and then the rest of the evening would be spent fielding questions from the students. I said my bit and then when the time came for the other professor to speak, his advice to the Asian-American students was that they should take their American-provided education and return "home" (Asia) to help Asia rise up and become the new world leader. America did

Understanding the Misunderstanding

not deserve their talents, he said, because it was too racist of a country and should not be allowed to benefit from their talents. Apparently, in his narrow view of the world, Asia did not have any racism, and so the students should return to the lands of "no racism"—which he reiterated was their "real" home—to apply their talents and presumably to punish America for its bad and racist ways.

I sometimes wish I were making this stuff up, but I'm not. I'm not sure I could make it up even if I wanted to. But let us return to the perverse paroxysm of pseudo-logic that my fellow professor—I struggle to use the word colleague—barked out on what should have otherwise been a cordial and productive discussion between professors with their wealth of experience and students in search of their own. I do understand the idea of academic freedom and am not suggesting in any way that such faculty should be censored: students should be exposed to any and all viewpoints and if our educational institutions have done their job the students should be well-equipped to sort trash from treasure. But just because someone has the academic freedom to speak their mind does not automatically mean that their mind contains things that should necessarily be spoken. But I digress.

To understand what this professor was suggesting on that evening, we need to return to the idea of the American Dream. The idea that the American Dream is a myth or a lie is partially a claim that the American Dream does not exist in reality, but it is also at the same time partially a claim that the American Dream *does* exist, but only for the dominant group in America. The American Dream was denounced and derided as the dream of someone else, and only for someone else—the privileged and dominant group of America, the White People. It was *their* dream, and to accept that dream was to assimilate to the group that was dominant, and thus to give in to the sources of one's own non-dominant oppression. Assimilation, and the idea of the American melting pot, became a subversive plot by the dominant group to control and erase the identities of everyone else—minorities and other marginalized groups. The preferred response of the new American rebel was thus to refuse and to reject anything that looked like assimilation. The resistance was born. To assimilate was to "sell-out," or to lose one's identity to the group that wanted to extirpate it in the first place, and so resistance to assimilation came in the form of separation. To resist the American Dream was to separate from it, and to denounce the American dream as a myth, or invent a new and alternative counter-dream. For the professor with whom I shared the podium that night, his dream for Asian-Americans was for them to take their American education and return "home" to Asia (note how this plays directly into the "perpetual foreigner" idea) and to share the benefits with their fellow Asians. The American Dream needed to be taken back to Asia—America no longer deserved it. It was time to steal the dream from those who did not deserve it and bring it to those who did. And to do so was, according to this other professor, a heroic act of resistance.

As for the students at the event, most of those present seemed confused at best—an encouraging sign, actually. The ambience in the room is what I would describe as awkwardly uncomfortable, though at least some of the students seemed susceptible to this so-called message of resistance, perhaps because it almost sounded like a positive thing. I mean, here was an Asian professor (originally from Asia), telling students to go "home" to a place that for most of them felt much less like home than America, and also telling them that not doing so and not going home was somehow a cowardly act of acquiescence and surrender. The fact that there was no consistently uniform response from the students in the room—some were intrigued, others were appalled—reveals a whole other layer to the idea of diversity in America that remains relatively unexplored. Sure, there might be more than one America—the phrase multi-America circulates quite widely—but if there is more than one America, how many Americas are there exactly? And more vexingly, is there one Asian-America, or many?

Little Americas
If those who claimed to have unmasked the "real" America by pointing out that it is really just an America of the dominant group—White America, as it were—and an America that pushes anything different off to the side and into the margins, then it does at least raise the question of whether this is unique or exceptional. Perhaps this is also true of all of these different groups that allegedly exist only at the margins of America. How else does one make a Latino community, except by creating and defining the dominant values of Latino-ness and asking everyone in the community to adopt them? How does one define the Asian-American community, except through the same process of dominance and assimilation? I have already discussed earlier the claim of many Asian-Americans that Filipinos could not be considered Asian because they were "too different," but doesn't this just repeat and emulate the exact same process that supposedly these marginalized groups are "resisting"? When this professor of ethnic studies told the Asian-American students to go back "home" to work for their respective race groups, the different reactions from the students showed a group of Asian-Americans who were clearly divided, who did not share any core set of values common to each and every student. Asian-America, it seems, was every bit as divided and diverse *within* itself as was America writ large. Yet our current version of diversity, and all the policies we have that are derived from it, has no way to account for and to address this internal sense of micro-diversity. What is more, this internal micro-diversity is often suppressed and censored by dominant actors *within* these communities for fear that any internal division or any internal diversity will weaken the community and its ability to wage resistance. And of course it would also weaken their own position as self-appointed

leaders and guardians of these communities. The problems of American diversity are replicated at every level of American society, and there is no way to fix the problems at one level without simultaneously fixing the problems at the others. One cannot fight and emulate oppression at the same time.

To clarify once again, what is not being argued here is that discrimination and racism and marginalization do not happen, or that diversity is just a bunch rhetorical nonsense. In fact, I am arguing that the problems of diversity stem from the fact that there is far more discrimination and racism and prejudice and marginalization in American than is commonly or properly acknowledged. All of these forms of injustice, ranging from the national and macro-level to the local and micro-level, have to be brought out into the open and given equal credence and equal concern for the destructive potential they each contain. Equality here means equal scrutiny.

To illustrate my point further, here are three separate vignettes offered as food for thought.

Vignette 1: A friend of mine from India arrived in Berkeley to begin her studies at UC Berkeley, and like all people who arrive in Berkeley for the first time, finding housing becomes the central focus of all thoughts and modes of existence, more important than food, sleep, and most bodily functions, with the possible exception of breathing. Students and other potential residents of Berkeley use almost any angle and tactic they can use to find a livable space in Berkeley, and quite often, those angles and tactics relate to issues of identity. It is a well-known but little-discussed reality of life in Berkeley that many apartment buildings or lease-holding tenants desire to offer their space only to persons of certain ethnic backgrounds. My friend from India, having difficulty finding an

Understanding the Misunderstanding

affordable space, finally thought she found a lucky break when she reached a landlord with a vacancy in his building. The landlord asked her: "Are you Asian?" (If you are wondering if this question is illegal the answer is yes, it is completely illegal, but it happens all the time.) In reply she said yes, and an appointment was then made to see the apartment. When she arrived, however, the landlord, who was ethnic Chinese (and from China), looked annoyed. "I thought you said you were Asian," he said. "I am," she said. "I am from South Asia. I am from India." The landlord looked at her and responded with scarcely concealed disdain: "That's not Asia. That's the third world." Not surprisingly, she did not get the apartment.

Vignette 2. A Filipino-American student came to my office to ask me about effective mobilization techniques for a new Filipino student organization she was hoping to start on campus. Like so many other student groups on campus that are based on race and ethnicity, the goal was to mobilize and galvanize the Filipino student community so they could multiply their power through numbers and advocate for Filipino-related issues. Also like so many other student groups, one of the primary goals was to gather together to "resist" the cultural hegemony of (white) American culture, in this case by fighting assimilation and learning to take pride in things that are Filipino. I pointed out the irony that there were numerous groups all around the Philippines, composed of local minority populations who were mobilizing around local languages and identities (such as Cebuano, Visayan, Ilocano, etc.) to resist the hegemony of the dominant Tagalog-speaking community in the Philippines. It took just as much assimilative pressure to make all of these groups Filipino as it did to make Filipinos into Americans. The student, who was a Tagalog-speaker, became very agitated. "Why do these minority groups have to make all this trouble?" she complained. "Can't they see that we should all just be Filipino?" For her, to "be Filipino" was to assimilate to the dominant Filipino culture, speak the dominant Filipino language (which was her language), and in essence, eliminate the diversity that exists among Filipinos. And why do this? So they could present a united front to resist assimilation in the United States and preserve their separate diversity. Apparently, Filipinos had to first assimilate in order to resist assimilation. The most striking thing in all of this was that the student saw nothing odd in this whatsoever—no irony, no paradox, no nothing.

Vignette 3. When the United States passed the first law in the country targeting and prohibiting online hate-speech, it was hailed as a powerful piece of progressive legislation that would protect minorities from the disturbing and rapidly-expanding trend that was becoming prevalent at the time, namely the racist hate-speech that was thriving in the unregulated playground of cyberspace. What took many people by surprise, however, was the identity of the perpetrator in the first major case prosecuted under the new law. In what was to be the first national case of successfully prosecuting someone for the commission of a hate crime on the internet, Richard J. Machado, a Latino student at the University of California, Irvine, was convicted in February 1998 of sending racially-motivated emails to Asian students, threatening them with death if they did not leave the school. The emails were signed with the epithet, "Asian Hater."[17] The case was prosecuted with a combination of the new federal law on online hate-speech and other civil rights legislation that was designed to break down the segregation that was so prevalent into the 1960s. The reason that the outcome was such a surprise to so many people, indeed a shock to some, was that it completely broke down the stereotypical architecture of hate-speech in any format: this was not some

---

17 For a more detailed account, see Davan Maharaj, "Anti-Asian E-Mail was Hate Crime, Jury Finds," *Los Angeles Times* (February 11, 1998) at http://articles.latimes.com/1998/feb/11/news/mn-17931

white guy wearing a white hood, sitting in his mom's basement, staring with pride at the confederate flag on the wall, spewing out racist invective and swilling down a mason jar of moonshine. It was someone from a group that until that moment could only be perceived, for some at least, as a *victim* of hate-speech, and never a perpetrator of it.

These three vignettes show clearly the crux of the problem with diversity in America: how can a nation composed of such a complex and intricate demographic cloth possibly find justice with a crude and simplistic vision of what ails us in our wounded identities? The idea of a Latino ranting against Asians is something that our current models and mindsets simply cannot process: it returns an eternal error message, the words translate into gibberish. Or we get contortionist semantic tricks that try to make this into a derivative act, a Latino made racist by the racist environment that oppresses him. But none of this is helpful, and none of it is true. These three vignettes are moments of racism and anti-diversity in America, and these moments come from a thousand different directions. Is there top-down, dominant-group racism in America (colloquially known as white racism)? Yes indeed, and only a troglodyte would deny it. But it is only one pitched battle in a much larger war, and you have to fight on every front to win that war, to create a new diversity that works for all and allows justice to prevail. Denial and blindness do nothing and help no one: you cannot fight what you cannot see, and you cannot see what you will not acknowledge. The first step toward making a diversity that works for everyone is to look at America anew: racism and prejudice and discrimination and hatred are everywhere, and they come in every color of the diversity rainbow. Racism and prejudice are always ugly, but without acknowledging the pervasiveness of the problem, it is as if we are spraying water on a few random embers on the lawn, while just behind us a forest fire is raging out of control.

Of course, this raises the question of why anyone wouldn't notice that forest fire in the first place and wouldn't want to turn their attention away from their own front yard. The most obvious reason for that is fear, fear that in this case stems from a variety of sources. There is the fear of being ousted by one's own group: if group solidarity and uniformity are seen as tactics of security and strength, then thinking differently or viewing things in a different way would render a person a threat to the rest of the group. There is also the fear of self-doubt: if the identity of the group is a pre-packaged set of values that defines who a person is, then stepping away from the group means having to build a new, yet untested identity. Better to stick with what is familiar, many would say, than venture into what is not. And then there is the fear that the conspiracy is true: the leaders of various minority communities in society—racial, ethnic, and others—often demand and expect conformity by all "members" to the shared values of the minority community because stepping away and thinking differently, they claim, is exactly what the so-called oppressor wants. It is easier for the oppressor to manipulate or destroy the lone individual than the unified group. If the conspiracy theory is right, turning away from the group and thinking differently could be a step toward self-destruction, or at least a willful leap into vulnerability. In reality, however, fear is one of the main things that keeps diversity from working.

Giving in to any or all of these fears comes at a huge price. Keeping our own yards safe while the rest of the world burns is hardly justifiable by any sense of cultural or social ethics, and the damage it ends up doing to the social fabric of diversity is in the long run counterproductive, self-destructive, and irreparable. Besides, this line of thinking has been a central part of the "diversification" of American society for the past two decades, and so far, all it has succeeded in doing is entrenching different peoples further and further into the comfort of their own groups and further and further away from each other. I don't think that's a productive vision of what diversity can and should do for a complex society like American society, or what it can and should do for any society, so perhaps it is time to rethink that sense of fear and transform it into something more positive. Why not invent a new type of diversity as an act of liberation, a leap of faith into a new sort of identity? Understandably, any leap of faith by definition contains an element of temerity, and this one is a big leap, to be sure. There is always the fear even here, too, of being the first to leap when no one else leaps with you or after you. Diversity, however, is one project that does not work unless everyone leaps into the unknown at the same time. The only incentive we have to make the leap is that playing it safe has not yet worked and most assuredly never will. Watering our lawns feels safe, but eventually the fire comes for us, too, whoever we are and wherever we are, and in that moment, we all get burned.

America: The land of no culture?
Aside from the intrinsic fear that seems to accompany identity-based issues, a fear that is often manifested in the form of brittle insensitivity, there is another reason often given for why groups tend to cluster together the way they do. This also brings us back to the central point of this part of the discussion, which is what America is and what else it should be or could be. I often hear people justify the "cliquishness" of identity groups in America on the grounds that America doesn't really have a culture of its own, and so it makes perfect sense that specific identity groups should keep to their own culture to retain a sense of identity. Part of this argument puts the cart before the horse—maybe America doesn't have a unified culture because people are too busy clinging to their separate subcultures—and so part of this argument seems just a

convenient act of self-justification for not really trying. If America does not have a bigger culture to jump into, then why not just stay put and avoid the leap of faith altogether? But if anything I have said in the preceding pages is true, and obviously I think it is or else I would not have said it, then it is more likely that these insular subcultures that so many people cling to are less like islands and more like life-rafts. Life-rafts were never meant to be permanent vessels; eventually, you'll have to reach land, or at least in the short term, a bigger boat. Building the bigger boat, or building the new land, is what the work of diversity is all about. The life rafts have done their work—it is time to let them go.

One of the first courses I ever taught was a seminar called "Asia on the Edge," which was a semester-long exploration of the various types of marginality—social, cultural, economic, political, and religious—that have existed and continue to exist in Asia. The last few weeks of the course looked at how these marginalities, and along with them the discrimination and the prejudice, that originated in Asia translated into and carried over into Asian communities in the United States. At the start of the semester, I asked each of the students—and they came from many different backgrounds—to write a few things about their identities, including a brief statement of how they identify themselves. One of the students in the course described herself rather straightforwardly as "Chinese-American" on that first day, and no doubt saw no reason to embellish or alter that description in any way. But as the semester moved along, and as each week brought a new set of readings on the disturbing consistency with which so many cultural groups in history find ways to justify their self-appointed dominance and supremacy (this is not just an American thing), this student came to the realization that "Chinese-American" was no longer an appropriate label. Instead, she began to see herself as "Hakka-American." The more this student learned about the long history of persecution and discrimination of the Hakka people in Chinese history, and the more she realized how the historical experience of the Hakka people differed significantly from the historical experience of the dominant ethnic Han group in China, the more she came to realize that being "Chinese-American" meant assimilating her own genealogical history into the dominant narrative of other, more dominant groups.

While I think this student's realization was an important learning moment in the context of the course, what I also found interesting was that another student in the course, who was (ethnic Han) Chinese-American, found this quite disturbing. Separating the category "Chinese-American" from "American" made perfect sense to him, as it reflected a separate experience of being American that was not a part of the mainstream American narrative, but to separate "Hakka" from "Chinese" was entirely unacceptable as it questioned what was in essence the dominant ethnic Han narrative of Chinese culture and history. In the former context, his own marginality had to be recognized in relation to America; in the latter, the marginality of others in relation to the "Chinese" part of "Chinese-American" had to be suppressed, eliminated, or assimilated. His inability to switch perspectives and recognize in others what we see clearly only in ourselves is one of the greatest flaws in our current discussions of diversity in America.

Similar examples can be found pretty much everywhere. In west Berkeley, for instance, there is a wonderfully delicious *chaat* (Indian snacks) house called Vik's that serves up various dishes from both northern and southern Indian cuisines. On any given day, the place is packed, and on any given weekend, even more so. I have had the good fortune to live in India, primarily in the south, and as a result, I consider southern Indian cuisine to be one of my comfort foods. Give me a masala dosa, a good bowl of sambar and a fiery chutney or two and I am as happy as I can be for a good, simple, comforting meal. This is one of the reasons I end up at Vik's on a regular basis. Over the years, I have had the chance to meet and talk with many of the patrons, striking up conversations as I wait for my name to be called at the counter. While the patrons of this establishment are a diverse crowd, by far the steadiest customer base consists of Indians who live in the area and who come by for an Indian meal, sometimes during the lunch rush, and most often on the weekends. I suppose there is nothing out of the ordinary about Indians eating Indian food in America, and for most people, they would not give it a second thought. But with my background and my experiences, and with the conversations I have had while I wait for my food at the counter of Vik's, there are things that do strike me as odd, things that once again, open up an interesting perspective on diversity in America.

When I lived in India, one of the most frequent complaints I would hear from Indians was that Americans (or Westerners in general) would come to India, and instead of adopting Indian cuisine as their standard diet, they would seek out Western-style restaurants and eat Western-style food. What is the point of coming to India, I would often hear, if you are not going to adapt to Indian ways? If you are going to just stick to your own culture, they would ask, why not just stay where you are? The expectation was clear: if you come to India, you should learn to appreciate and eat Indian food—curry, dosa, idli, and everything else. Yet when the situation is put into reverse, and there are crowds of Indians driving through the insanity of Bay Area traffic to eat Indian food and stock up on Indian groceries (just as Americans would go to Western-style supermarkets in India), those complaints are rejected out of hand. An Indian in America who eats Indian food on a regular basis is doing so, as I have been told repeatedly, because it is part of his or her culture, part of her or his identity. So what then of the Americans who are eating American food in India? That is different, goes the explanation, because America, once again, "has no culture."

I also hear a related comment over and over again: "There is no such thing as American cuisine." Since America has no culture and no cuisine of its own, there can be no expectations on Indians or anyone else to partake in that culture or cuisine. On the other hand, since India supposedly has a strong culture and a distinct cuisine, Americans and Westerners in India are obliged to assimilate to local ways. Somehow, Indians eating Indian food in America represents their "culture," but Americans eating American food in India represents their "ignorance," or even "arrogance." Clearly, something can't be right here.

The inability to see through both sides of the cultural window, to notice only the habits of others and not to be aware of the way that image of others reflects back on ourselves, is part of the fractured image that restrains diversity from being what it was meant to be in America. Because of the time I spent living in India, I am absolutely familiar with pretty much every type of Indian dish there is: I know what it is, I know what it is made from, I know what region it is from, and I know the proper ("Indian") way to eat it. If I am at a place like Vik's, invariably someone will notice this, perhaps that I am eating my dosa with my hands (as would be normal in India), and I will suddenly have the conversation that starts with something like: "Wow, you seem to know Indian food well!" I don't mind the question, and it usually leads to a longer conversation about my time in India, my food preferences, and many other related and sometimes not-so-related things. What makes me *want* to mind the question, however, is the premise behind the question and how it mimics the situation I discussed earlier. The question is based on the following line of reasoning: someone from India sees me, they see that I am a person who by appearance does not look like someone who is from India (though how do they know for sure?), so how could I be eating food in a way that appears to be Indian? Now let's switch a few things around and rephrase the question and the setting: someone who is American sees someone who looks like they are from India, and who by appearances does not look like they are from America (how do they know for sure?), and so decides to start a conversation by making the observation: "Wow, you speak really good English!" For some reason, pointing out that I can eat Indian food like it is eaten in India, assuming from my appearance alone that I would not be able to do so, is a perfectly valid observation to make, but pointing out that someone can speak very good English, assuming from their appearance that they would not be able to do so, is considered yet another reason as to why America is "so racist."

It strikes me as utterly incongruent with the project of diversity that these situations could not both be seen as similarly constructive moments: when I tell someone from India how and why I can eat Indian food the way I do, he or she learns another example of how Indian culture can be equally shared and appreciated by non-Indians; when someone from India (or any other place) explains they can speak English because they learned it at school in India, or because they were born in America to a family that immigrated from India, then one more American learns that speaking English is a skill shared far beyond his or her normal set of expectations. I suppose next time I am eating my meal at Vik's and someone from India points out that I know how to eat Indian food, I could throw my food on the floor and run off to find a group of friends who look just like me and complain about how Indians are "so racist." But really, how would that help or solve anything? What possible contribution could that make to the cultivation of an integrated, shared, diverse society? And how simple-minded and petulant would I have to be to see my reaction as an act of "resistance"?

There is no use counting how many Americas there are, and it seems wasted energy that detracts more than it intrigues. There are so many different models and metaphors that get tossed around like so many ideological pizzas. Is America a melting pot? Is it a patchwork quilt? Is it a mosaic? Is it a mosaic of quilts melted in a pot? None of them bring us to that point of arrival, where we understand what America is, though each in its own way brings us closer. Yet I do think it is something of a cop out to argue that the lack of clarity somehow translates into a lack of culture, especially when the argument is made in the context of encouraging the myriad communities that exist in America to stick to their own cultural life rafts. Only the most extravagant imbecile extols the beauty of his own little island to mask the fact that he never learned to swim.

The narcissism of identity politics
When Barack Obama was first elected president in November 2008, one of the phrases that began to flow from the mouths of many was that finally, America had a president who "looks like me." I was puzzled by this phrase then, and I am still puzzled by this phrase now. I suppose it could mean a lot of different things, but what puzzled me most was not so much the meaning of the phrase. No, what puzzled me was why this was important at all. There have been forty-five presidents since the first presidency of George Washington, and as far as I can tell, absolutely none of them look like me. In some cases, I am grateful for that, while in others I am just relieved. I do understand that much of the underlying idea here is that President Obama is, well, not white, which means we have that first moment in American history when the presidency and diversity meet, mingle, and meld in the euphoric amphitheater of political transformation. But there is also an unsettling sense of deeply embedded narcissism in the sentiment that all of us should expect or desire at some point a president who "looks like me" (which says nothing about whether the president "thinks like me") and that somehow this is an effective or acceptable litmus test for the quality of American democracy and diversity. What the president looks like, as it turns out, is irrelevant.

To be imbued with the positive warmth of approval because the president "looks like me" is in fact the most superficial standard of evaluation imaginable. At the most basic level, it could be interpreted as a statement by African-Americans that having a black president makes them feel included in America in a way that has never happened previously. If that is the case, then what does this say about the diversity of the rest of America? Even if we could simplify American society down to one hundred different categories of identity, it would mean that it would take another four hundred years for all Americans to feel they have had a president that looks like them, assuming nothing but one-term presidencies and assuming that each election selects a candidate from a different ethnic group. But should we really accept the premise that for instance the Hmong community in America will never feel like they belong in America until there is a Hmong president? There is a substantial Sri Lankan community in California, but they consist of both Tamil and Sinhalese persons. Would we need a Tamil president and then a Sinhalese one before they can feel at home in America? Again, what the president looks like or who looks like the president are both irrelevant.

We can also consider the converse: if President Obama does not "look like me," is he therefore not my president? This way of thinking also gets us nowhere fast. Intertwined with this idea of a predilection for a president whose appearance is as close to mine as possible is the assumption that a president who looks like me will also act like me and think like me. That is, there is an assumption that people who are from the same identity group will not have any diversity among themselves, that each and every black president would have the same set of values and same type of opinions, and every black person in America would share those values and opinions. Think of how many times you may have heard African-Americans criticize Obama for not being "black enough" as president. This harkens back to the same unproductive situation discussed earlier in which groups that clamor for diversity at the macro level actually suppress diversity at the micro level, and groups who oppose assimilation to larger American society demand assimilation within their own. When these identity-based expectations do not pan out, when appearances do not match actions, the result is one of disappointment and disorientation. When the president who "looks like me" is not acting and making decisions "like me," disillusionment sets in. After so much talk in the realm of diversity that being a "person of color" was such a fundamentally different way of seeing the world—prone to justice, prone to resistance, prone to fixing the things that non-color people broke—we finally get a president "of color" and the shock of the century is that his color and appearance make no difference at all. The same will be true, I suspect, if and when we finally get a female president in the United States.

The reason for that is not, as some would have it, that "the system is white" and so nonwhite persons have no choice but to "become white" if they want to succeed. Nor is it that "the system is male," and so women have no choice but to conform to the male-dominated culture of politics. No, the reason is that the whole premise of wanting a president who "looks like me" is flawed in the first place. The preferable quest is to find a president who "thinks like me," regardless of color and all other markers of identity, or even better, a president who just "thinks different" or "acts different." Diversity is supposed to stop us from making choices and prejudgments based on superficial characteristics. If we are still looking for a president who "looks like me," then we still have a long, long way to go before diversity starts becoming a substantive part of American democracy.

What America needs is more of me
The desire to see more and more people like ourselves in every conceivable nook and cranny of public and private life is what

fuels the narcissism that undermines any gain that diversity policy and practice may have achieved. Diversity is supposed to *cure* our narcissism, but as it is currently configured, it rewards it. Many advocates of our current strains of diversity policy argue that the gains of diversity are undermined because the old dominant order ("whites") is still too deeply entrenched and so more diversity has to be applied in order for identity-based injustice and inequality to be uprooted once and for all. To apply more diversity in this case means largely to add more and more people from the advocate's identity group. *Add more of me, and other people that look like me, and eventually justice will occur.* But justice does not occur, not because there are not yet enough of "people like me," but because the whole exercise is delusional and self-defeating. If President Obama is a different kind of president, it is because he is the individual known as Barack Obama, and not because he is black. Trying to fit the person back into the category is usually the first ugly step towards stereotyping. Put differently: There are approximately 39 million black persons currently in the United States, and all that means is that there are approximately 39 million different ways to be a black president. Anyone who thinks or expects otherwise is engaging in a wistful soliloquy on the sound of their own voice. *Diversity is not about learning to adore the song you sing; it is about listening to the songs of others.*

The presidency is of course one thing, and perhaps an idiosyncratic one at that, so what about this narcissism in the broader perspective, in the more common spaces where common people live? How does it play out in these other spaces, and what does it do, or not do, for diversity? For starters, we can once again borrow that time machine and go back to the not-too-distant past to a moment when it seemed that everything about diversity was under threat. In the summer of 1997, the campus at UC Berkeley's law school, then called Boalt Hall, was in an uproar over the composition of the incoming class at the law school, the first since the implementation of Proposition 209. Prop 209 created a ban on racial preferences as a determining factor for university admissions. The law school campus, like other campuses around the country, was in something of an uproar because the banning of racial preferences in admissions had led to what was seen as an immediate "loss" of diversity, at least according to the perceptions of some observers. Fourteen African-American students had been admitted to the incoming law school class, but all fourteen had declined and had accepted offers to other schools. This meant that the incoming law school class had only one African-American student, who had been admitted for the previous year's class (before Proposition 209 came into effect) but had deferred his legal studies for one year. What I find most intriguing about the situation is the commentary that emerged around this issue, mostly for what it says about different viewpoints on what diversity was supposed to do or was expected to do.

One observer noted, for instance, in relation to the fact that only one African-American student was in the entering law school class: "Can you imagine the pressure of being the only one?"[18] The first counter-response I would offer to this question is: what pressure could there possibly be? The question seems to be based on the belief that, once again, outward appearance determines inward demeanor. In other words, an African-American student is admitted because he or she will represent the "black" point of view. It won't be because they are an expert on the history of Marvel comics, or because they are a master chef in Mongolian cuisine, or because they have a deep and compelling interest in income tax law. No, it will be because at law school, they are expected to perform "blackness"—speak it, act it, and be it at all times—and other students will see this and learn about "blackness" through

---

18 For a contemporary account, see Pamela Burdman, "Boalt Law's Entering Class Has Only 1 Black," *SFGate* (June 28, 1997) at http://www.sfgate.com/news/article/Boalt-Law-s-Entering-Class-Has-Only-1-Black-2820029.php

the diversity it supposedly presents. This is a very strange pressure indeed: to expect the one African-American student to represent the entire African-American community. In essence, the student was expected to be a stereotype of his own community. Just as there were those who expected Obama to "be black" as a black president, so too were there many who felt that as a black law student, this one person had to always remember to "be black," and more importantly, to be nothing else.

I find the assumption demeaning to African-Americans, who are in this type of scenario assumed to have only one collective viewpoint, which they should all follow and believe, and I find the assumption demeaning to the one African-American student, whose whole complex identity as a person has been distilled down into one grotesquely simplified element, namely his ability to "be black" or "act black." In the same year that this was happening at UC Berkeley, one African-American student had been admitted to the University of Texas at Austin School of Law, which had also just initiated a ban on racial preferences, but had declined admission once he had learned that he was going to be the only black student. Although some had opined that this was the beginning of a new era of segregation in America, there was one crucial difference between the original days of segregation in America and what was happening now: the element of choice. These were not students who were being denied admission to law school or being told they had to attend separate law schools. They were students who were *choosing* to go to other law schools. This then leads to the important question: why?

One disturbing clue emerges from a comment made by a Latino student who had been offered admission to the law school at UC Berkeley but had chosen to attend Columbia Law School instead. Chief among the reasons this student cited for his decision was this: "I want to be around other Latinos." Here is where the narcissism of diversity reveals its true capacity to undermine diversity's own potential. In my earlier discussion of the *Grutter* Supreme Court case, I pointed out the belief among administrative officials at the University of Michigan that racial preferences were necessary in order to ensure the "critical mass" of diversity among the entering class at their law school. The problem is that the ideal of the "critical mass" and the reality of what actually happens move in opposite directions. The reality of the "critical mass" idea is that students from specific identity groups seek out other students from the same identity group, and if there is sufficient "critical mass" they can form a micro-community, in essence an enclave, that circulates very little or not at all with other identity groups. The statement "I want to be around other Latinos" shows this clearly. The critical mass idea is an illusion, and the "robust exchange of ideas" promised by proponents of the critical mass idea never occurs.

By this reckoning of diversity, the goal of diversity policies in law school admissions is to admit a sufficient number of students from each identity group so that members of those groups can *avoid* diversity by insulating themselves with the sameness of their own group. Here is the crucial difference between diversity as *being different* versus *understanding difference*: if we are crafting admissions policies so that Latinos can be with Latinos, blacks can be with blacks, and so on, then we are merely crafting the illusion of diversity without offering any substance behind it. For a Latino to want to be and get to be "around other Latinos" does not strengthen diversity at all. It evades it. And that is precisely why our diversity policies keep failing to produce the results we hope for and expect.

The involution of America
When I have to wear my academic cap—which looks a lot like a dunce cap only it has the phrase "I is 2 smart" embroidered on it—I refer to the process by which persons of a particular identity group use diversity as an excuse to turn inward and seek out sameness and homogeneity as *involution*. Involution is probably the greatest threat to any set of diversity policies, no matter how

carefully crafted they may appear to be. It comes in many forms and it stems from many sources and practices, but if we want diversity to move in a more constructive direction, we will need to re-craft and re-forge those policies to encourage and reward people to *resist* the narcissistic inertia of involution and instead seek out and understand difference, which it seems to me is the true promise of diversity. In that sense, being the only African-American student in the entering law school class should not be seen as any sort of "pressure" or any sort of negative experience. As the only student from one particular group, this is probably the best possible scenario for diversity to work its magic: pre-empted from any sort of involution, since there is no one else from the same group to seek out and cling to—no ethnic or racial life rafts—the only student from one particular group has no choice but to experience and understand difference no matter where he or she turns. Every person they meet will offer something different and something new, just as they will offer something different and new in return, and in the struggle to comprehend and understand what is everywhere different and unfamiliar, diversity will finally have had a chance to reveal its promise and evolve its potential.

As an example of the type of mindset that involution produces, I offer the homepage of UC Berkeley's very own *Berkeley La Raza Law Journal*, which, like most law school-produced law journals, is run by students at the law school.[19] For those not familiar with the term *La Raza*, it is a Spanish word that is used to refer to persons of Hispanic/Latino heritage in a way that invokes pride and group belonging. A quick glance at the home page for *La Raza Law Journal* (at least as of this writing) will reveal an image of people united and marching through the streets of what looks like

---

19 At the time of publication, this image has been removed from the home page of the journal, found at http://www.boalt.org/LRLJ

Understanding the Misunderstanding

a village, accompanied by the slogan "*El Pueblo unido jamás será vencido*" (A people united will never be vanquished). Considering the previous discussion about how America is racist because it assumes that nonwhite people don't speak English, it is an odd thing indeed to have a homepage for an American group whose slogan is in Spanish only (no English translation is provided). The other interesting thing about the website is that all of the faces in the image of the marching protesters—it is a drawing rather than a photograph—are intentionally made dark to show that the people who are united are non-white and would not include whites. The message is clear: this is us and everything you see here is only for us—if you are not one of us, then you can admire us but never join our group. That, in essence, is what involution looks life: insiders stick together, outsiders are kept out.

The tricky part about involution is that it is quite often invisible unless you know what to look for and where to find it. At the simplest level, I can watch the process happen in my classroom almost as if it were a time-lapse movie. On the first day of class in a large lecture hall, there will simply be a large number of students, most of them distracted by the shock and confusion of the first day of the semester, but all of them focused on the content of the course at hand. By the second week, students will have scanned the classroom looking for familiar faces, and by the third week I notice the trend that students from the same identity group have started to sit together—the life raft forms. It is not entirely universal—that is, there are always students whose friendships are based on shared interest rather than shared heritage. But those students are in the minority, pun actually intended. For most, however, there is the familiar and disturbing pattern by which ever so slowly, Latinos will cluster with Latinos, black will cluster with blacks, and so forth.

This process also works in assignments, particularly in those involving a choice of topic. Even if I give students complete freedom in choosing the topics of their papers, the topics of these papers are usually driven by identity involution. It gets to the point where, for instance, if a Korean or Korean-American student comes into my office to discuss the topic of their research paper, I can guess with around 98% accuracy what their proposed topic will be. The topic will almost always be something about Korea: why the world should help North Korea refugees, why Japan is wrong about everything and needs to be punished, why the two Koreas should be reunited, why K-pop (Korean pop music) is better than all other forms of music ever created by humans throughout history, and so forth. If I hazard to suggest a different sort of topic, something that requires more diversity of thought—for example writing about the equally sad plight of refugees in an entirely different part of the world, or something about the prejudice against non-Korean refugees in South Korea itself—the response will be one of bewilderment and confusion. Invariably the student will admit they have no interest in those "other issues" and will stick to their choice of a topic that is as close to their own identity as possible. This works for nearly every identity group, and here I am only using Korean identity as an example. But regardless of the groups I choose, the end result will be the same. In essence, my class will look diverse, but there is very little substantive diversity actually going on.

There are many other ways that the processes of involution and narcissism work together under the banner of diversity in the educational institutions of America. One of the reasons that so many students support diversity as it is currently practiced is because of the way they first encounter it: after arriving on campus, students often join identity-based student groups, either by being recruited by students already in those groups or sometimes by being encouraged by their parents, who want them to stay as much as possible within their own cultural or ethnic group, lest college undo so many years of cultural and ethnic upbringing. I am often amused by the students who do the recruiting on campus for these student groups. They stand in the public areas of campus as crowds of students go by and simply look for someone who looks like they are from the same group (and note again how this act of "diversity" is really an act of sameness and homogeneity—recruiters are scanning the crowds looking only for familiar and similar faces, so if you look different, you're irrelevant). What amuses me is how often they get it wrong: a black student group hands a flyer to a student, only for the student to say, "I'm Indian!," or a Chinese student group hands a flyer to a student, only for the student to say, "I'm Mongolian!" But if the recruitment is successful, or if the student voluntarily joins (on their own accord or through parental request, etc.), what they discover is in essence a pre-packaged community and an automatic sense of belonging. Gone is the anxiety of having to make new friends in an unfamiliar place; now those friends are all there waiting for you, and even more comforting, they are friends who "look like me," if me is you. And since one of the things student groups do on campuses is advocate for the interests of their group—promoting diversity by wanting more of their own homogeneous group on campus—that version of diversity becomes the dominant one. Diversity and friendship and politics all roll together in one bizarre artificial concoction of sameness and homogeneity. Involution has been confused with diversity, and as a result, diversity fails.

In these circumstances, diversity looks as easy as it looks good: diversity provides instant friends and pre-packaged "networks" and the only work required is to embrace one's own group identity. Note that nothing in this process requires students to understand or explore anything other than themselves, another perversion of the idea of diversity. If I introduce the topic of diversity into any of my classes, especially in a critical context, there is almost immediate pushback, because diversity is for them beyond question. Most students have this positive experience—pre-packaged groups of friends, and so on—and the idea that something might be wrong with it is a very threatening and uncomfortable suggestion. If a student belongs to one of these student groups, or at least to a networked community of sameness, none of the problems inherent with our current diversity practices will be apparent; they will remain invisible, or will be cloaked in the positivity of the student's experience with diversity, or else will be justified as necessary acts of resistance against the hegemony, exploitation, discrimination, and manipulation of the dominant group in contemporary America. If I start questioning diversity in a crowd of students, it will be interpreted as a threat: either I am trying to take away their friends, or I am trying to undermine their cultural or ethnic identity, or I am just trying to dominate as best I can. Anyone who questions the way things are is the enemy. Diversity as it is must be left unquestioned and unchallenged, even as it fails extravagantly all around us.

An interesting experiment
One of the projects I have often introduced into classes in order to break through the cloak of invisibility is to first introduce a whole new concept of diversity—where diversity is not about *being different* but about *understanding difference*—and then ask any student who is interested to volunteer for an experiment that exemplifies this different approach to diversity. Several of my students have taken up the challenge and their experiences were a crash-course in the vital life lesson of how-things-are-never-as-they-seem. The experiment goes like this.

For a Chinese-American student to join a Chinese-American student group, or any other group relating to Chinese culture, is the easiest thing in the world. But what rule says that Chinese-Americans can only be a part of Chinese cultural and social activities? If diversity is supposed to help us understand and appreciate other cultures and other people who are different from ourselves, then how does joining a group based on sameness and then relishing the sensation of sameness further that goal? The experiment I offered came in the form of a challenge to experience diversity by crossing the cultural line. The first student who volunteered was a Chinese-American student, and so, she set off to answer the question, What would happen if a Chinese-American student wanted to join a Latino student group? Not surprisingly, most student groups that think they are a part of the project of diversity have very little interest in actually practicing diversity. My Chinese-American student found that time after time, there was real discomfort with the idea of crossing identity boundaries, and she was repeatedly turned away and told to find another group and to "stick with her own kind." The same groups who were most vocal in proclaiming that *the American dream is theirs not mine* elided effortlessly into the refrain of *this is our student group not yours.*

With very, very few exceptions, every student of mine who has embraced this challenge has met with a similar response. Student groups that complain that "America does not accept us because we are different" have no problem rejecting students outside their identity group because they are, well, different. Even at UC Berkeley, a campus whose students pride themselves on radicalism and progressivism and of course on being at the forefront of the struggle for diversity, the same results occur. Two years ago, one of my students took up this challenge as her personal project, and would come to my office on a regular basis to tell me of her experiences (I still keep in touch with her). Her interactions with student groups whose primary purpose for existence relates to the identity of its members pretty much repeat the same experience I first saw over ten years ago. To my mind, she embodied the best of what diversity could offer: an Iranian-American with a passion for break-dancing and K-pop, with study abroad experience in China, Taiwan, and Costa Rica.

Again, however, when she tried to practice diversity in a meaningful way, she encountered only the awkwardness, the discomfort, the stick-with-your-own-kind mentality. One group actually admitted to her that they don't actually do anything, but are simply a social group for people who are from a specific part of Asia (the group included Asians and Asian-Americans, so again, note the slippage between those two categories). They get together to talk about how great their "home" culture is and go out to local restaurants to eat food from that region. They pretty much told my student that because she was from "someplace else" she should find a different group.

What all of these experiences show clearly, and what my students have come to learn in a very painful and eye-opening way, is that discrimination and exclusion are not what the dominant group does to everyone else. It is what *everyone* does to everyone else. No one notices these anomalies because our current working idea about what diversity is, and the policies and practices that derive from that idea, are all deeply flawed. Students—and I should add not just students but most people in general—think that preserving and practicing their own culture is the work of diversity. It is not: what it cultivates is narcissism, not diversity. It is that narcissism that encourages students to spend their time in class looking for people who are the same rather than looking out for those who are different. Just as I don't think it makes much sense to spend our lives waiting for a president who "looks like me," I don't think it serves the cause of diversity any better to spend time in a classroom looking for another student who "looks like me."

Speaking to ourselves and avoiding others
Aside from these general experiences that can and often do happen in any classroom, it is also worth the time to understand how specific programs designed to expose students to diverse environments are circumvented or manipulated in ways that undermine their intent and effect altogether. Take, for instance, the standard requirement of many universities that students must take at least two years of a foreign language. I fully support this requirement,

for reasons that should be obvious at this point, and I often get annoyed when departments waive the requirement or allow students to test out of it or accept a student's "heritage language" as a foreign language. Nothing represents the challenge of walking in someone else's shoes, of seeing the world through their eyes, like studying a foreign language. Yes, students often complain about this requirement (when will I ever use this language?), and sometimes parents complain about it, too (when will my child ever use this language?), but these complaints miss the point entirely. Two years of language study will not make you fluent in any language, and much of what you learn will disappear within a few years unless you continue to use or practice the language. Everyone knows that. But even if that happens, the one thing you will not forget is the struggle of trying to master something that is truly outside your comfort zone, of being forced to express yourself in a totally different way, of trying to understand how a native speaker of that language sees the same thing you see but chooses a whole different vocabulary and mode of expression to describe it. That part of the learning experience is the invaluable part. To miss that part of an education is to miss one of the most fundamental aspects of what diversity can do to enhance education. It is one of the things that pushes education beyond something that is merely functional to something that is truly transformational.

It is for this reason that I get so upset to watch students do everything they can, including outright deceit, to find a way to bypass or minimize the educative potential of learning a foreign language. There are two ways this happens. The first is by choosing a language that is as close to their own identity as possible, thereby minimizing the experience of diversity and the struggle with difference that is central to the whole process. A student of Swedish descent, for instance, who grew up in a household where Swedish was somewhat familiar (perhaps their parents or grandparents spoke Swedish) and where Swedish ways of thinking were also familiar might choose to take Swedish as a foreign language. In this case, the diversity potential of studying a foreign language is minimized. The second way in which students bypass or minimize the potential that foreign language study offers is by taking a language they *already* know, sometimes fluently. When I was a graduate student, for instance, one of the languages I studied was Hindi. When I began my studies, it did not take long to realize that well over half the students in the class were already fluent Hindi speakers, either because they were from India or from Hindi-speaking families of Indian descent, and they were clearly taking the class for the easy A. The point for them was to avoid "wasting time" in studying something new and challenging. Students can do this because they can lie to the university about how much of the language they actually know, and because the university has no way to test if that claim is true or not. You would think that language instructors would be on the lookout for students who clearly already know the language they are supposedly trying to learn, but what often happens instead—and I have seen this first-hand—is that language instructors, who are usually hired because they are native speakers, recognize other native speakers more as compatriots from the same identity group rather than students who are circumventing the educational requirement. I remember sitting in my Hindi language class while students conversed with the instructor about different places in India where they had been and where their family came from and how their father would use this word for something but their mother would use some other word, pretty much leaving the handful of us that were in the class actually to learn the language feeling completely left out. Involution at work.

Another university program that is specifically set up to expose students to a diverse living experience is the study abroad program, sometimes known as EAP (Education Abroad Program). Here, too, students often take advantage of the program to get academic credit for something that misses the whole point of a program like EAP and seems to avoid or minimize the diversity that the experience of studying abroad is supposed to provide. One extreme example of this, for instance, was a student from Mexico who came to UC Berkeley and then applied for the EAP program—to study in Mexico. Why would a student do this? In this case, the student could receive academic credit at Berkeley for returning home to be with family and friends, and also manage to avoid any kind of diversity by using a program designed ironically to promote diversity.

Many other students also apply to the EAP program to experience more sameness than difference, or more often, to embrace and celebrate their identity group by traveling to the "homeland." By far the majority of Korean-American students, for instance, choose to go to South Korea to study for their EAP experience. There are many reasons for this. Many Korean-American students I have spoken with have made it clear that their parents encouraged them to choose Korea. In one case, a Korean-American student told me her parents would not pay for her to go to any other "foreign" place. Many of these students still have relatives in Korea, so as with the student from Mexico, it is a bit like going home to visit family but getting college credit to do so. Another reason for choosing to go to Korea is peer pressure: since most Korean-American students choose to go to Korea, it becomes a very alluring and comforting blanket of sameness to be in Korea at the same time with others who are from the same identity group. Still another reason is that Korean universities actively engage in the project of bringing Korean-American students "home" (from a South Korean perspective, Korean-Americans are often seen as Koreans who live in a different country, away from their proper home).

Again, all of this flies in the face of the very purpose of studying abroad. What the EAP experience should be is one in which a Korean-American student goes to a place like Iceland or Bolivia: nothing is familiar, and the food and the language are equally foreign. The challenge of studying abroad is to put oneself in an entirely unfamiliar environment and then learn to adjust to a whole different way of living, thinking, and seeing. This is what diversity is supposed to be, and this is the opportunity that diversity is supposed to offer. If we are instead sending Korean students to Korea, Mexican students to Mexico, Indian students to India, all we are doing is circumventing the experience and offering an education in narcissism. When a Korean-American student goes to Korea to study, it only strengthens the involution process, since whatever new friendships emerge out of the experience will be only with other Koreans or Korean-Americans. And given the undercurrent of anti-Americanism that is popular among Korean students at universities in Korea, most of it based on ignorance and misinformation, many Korean-Americans return from the EAP experience with the idea that Korea is some sort of superlative utopia—one Korean-American student in my class boasted that it was "the best country in the world" after his experience there—a conclusion they reach largely because they have not had to negotiate or struggle with any meaningful sense of diversity during the whole experience. What was supposed to be an education into the challenges of diversity instead becomes a narcissistic celebration of the pleasures of ethnic homogeneity.

Diversity in civic space
At this point, it would be easy to assume that these examples are not necessarily indicative of any sort of larger trend since college students are not the most representative sample of the population. And to a certain extent that might be true. College students, and especially the wonderfully quirky students of UC Berkeley, can be as peculiar and odd as a two-toed sloth in a three-toed town (read that joke slowly for maximum effect). But of course, college students eventually graduate—most of them, at least—and they take the attitudes and perspectives they learn in college with them on

Understanding the Misunderstanding

the trajectory of the rest of their lives. For that reason alone, it is crucial that diversity be set right because it becomes one of those experiences that has life-long consequences. But the narcissism that is so prevalent on college campuses as a product of identity politics and unimaginative diversity programs is not unique to college campuses, and can be found pretty much anywhere anyone is willing to look for it.

Take, for instance, the unexpected case of the tiny Sichuan peppercorn. In 1968, the US Department of Agriculture banned the import of Sichuan peppercorns, because they are the dried berry of a particular citrus bush that potentially carries a canker that could spread to other citrus plants in the United States and thus wipe out a large part of the citrus industry, particularly in California and Florida. In other words, it had the potential to destroy a large part of the agricultural economy of America. When the Department of Agriculture began to get stricter about enforcing the ban in 2002, the peppercorns did not necessarily disappear, but instead just went through their own sort of involution. Because the peppercorns are an essential ingredient in Sichuan cuisine (Sichuan being a part of China), the most likely place to find the peppercorns was in Chinese grocery stores. And so, an ethical quandary emerged: was it more important to bypass the ban so that your Sichuan food in America could taste like it does in China, or was it more important to protect the citrus industry, which forms a central part of the American agricultural economy? A quick walk through grocery stores in the Chinatowns in San Francisco and Oakland showed the answer of at least some shop owners: Sichuan peppercorns remained for sale, but were simply unlabeled or intentionally mislabeled. Only "proper" Chinese people would know where they were and how to find them. When a Mandarin-speaking reporter was investigating the availability of the peppercorns in Oakland's Chinatown, she learned that they were secretly available behind the counter, though the clerk made it clear she would not have sold them to any English-speaking, non-Chinese customer.[20] In a different shop in San Francisco's Chinatown, the reporter was told by the shop clerk: "Even here, I am not selling any to foreigners." What I love about the latter quote is how utterly ambiguous it is. Does it mean, as with the Oakland shop owner, that "foreigners" are non-Chinese? Does it mean that American citizens who enter Chinatown are foreigners, unless they are ethnic Chinese? Does it mean the clerk can glance at a person and tell whether they are "foreign" or not? It doesn't take a brain trust to see the imbricated layers of involution, exclusion, narcissism, and discrimination that are at work here. And note that right here in America, at least according to this story, ethnic Chinese are perfectly capable of treating non-Chinese with the same exclusion and "foreignness" that many Chinese-Americans have complained about in their own experience in America.

I've experienced similar moments of exclusiveness that amount to a form of discrimination in Chinatown. I've been out to dinner countless times with Chinese friends, and more often than not, we end up with a dish that isn't on the menu. It turns out to be a dish that the chef makes only for people who know to ask for it, and also know how to ask for it—in fluent Mandarin. Non-Chinese guests to the restaurant are not told that this dish exists (often they are specialties of the chef and so are quite delicious) and so it's almost as if there is a certain part of the restaurant that may as well have a sign that says "Chinese Only" or "Non-Chinese Not Allowed." I've also had the experience where Chinese customers were allowed to pay with credit cards but non-Chinese customers were told "cash only." The latter situation is slightly different from the first. Many restaurants in Chinatown (and in other areas as well) prefer cash

---

20 See Denise Landis, "Sichuan's Signature Fire is Going Out. Or is it?" *The New York Times* (February 4, 2004) at http://www.nytimes.com/2004/02/04/dining/sichuan-s-signature-fire-is-going-out-or-is-it.html

only because they don't have to pay the fees to the credit card companies and can also underreport their earnings and thus pay lower taxes (this is not a practice unique to Chinese-American businesses). Still, to allow this service for "special" customers (those with the right ethnic background) and to deny it to others is blatant discrimination. Think about it: if you were in a restaurant where white customers could pay with a credit card but all non-whites had to pay in cash, would there be any other way to describe it other than discrimination?

Making the right connections
Diversity is supposed to open our eyes to the connections and similarities we ourselves have with others, both positive and negative, but instead what we have created are blinders of narcissism that conveniently prevent us from seeing that these are collective issues and shared challenges. We are too busy complaining that *they* don't want to walk in our shoes to notice that *we* don't want to walk in theirs.

The blindness of narcissism is as counterproductive as it is corrosive. I don't know how many times I have engaged in conversations with Chinese-Americans about the history of discrimination against Chinese-Americans in America, and yet in the same conversation, if the issue of discrimination against Tibetans in China comes up, suddenly this is considered a Western myth—no such discrimination exists, I am told. It is a mystery how a person can focus so intensively on one and then remain willfully blind to the other, and yet this is precisely the sort of thing that our current models of diversity encourage and reward. And that would be fine, if we want diversity to be a useless waste of time that allows us to decry and lament the discrimination we have experienced from others and then cover up and hide the discrimination we engage in ourselves. But it seems to me that diversity should be something else altogether, something that genuinely allows us to understand ourselves among others, something that lets us see ourselves and see others with the same perception and the same perspicacity.

Here again is another example of how this is clearly not happening. At a discussion on Korean-related issues held at UC Berkeley in April 2010, I was invited to give a lecture and chose to give my lecture on the discrimination faced by migrant workers and other marginalized populations in South Korea. Migrant workers in South Korea face constant discrimination and are often exploited for their labor, with little recourse for justice. At the end of my talk the format moved to a question-and-answer session, and here are the first two questions I received, both from Korean-American students. The first one: "Since these minorities create trouble for the Korean people and statistically are more likely to commit crimes and be violent, you can't really call it discrimination, can you? Isn't it more like the Korean people just protecting themselves?" And here is the second one, in its entirety: "Can't we blame the Americans for all of this?" The stupefying part, again, is the evocative blindness that prevents both Koreans and Korean-Americans from seeing what is right in front of their eyes in Korea, while at the same time they have no problem attributing such things to America.

We can have a bit of impish fun with these questions to show just how ugly they are. Suppose we are at a different event, only this time the topic is the rising crime rate in Los Angeles. Now suppose at the end of a talk on the dramatic rise in crime in certain neighborhoods of Los Angeles, someone asks the question, without the slightest hint that there is anything inappropriate with the question: "Can't we blame the Mexicans for that?" or even, "Can't we blame the illegals for that?" Even someone who had just had their brains eaten in a zombie apocalypse buffet could see how racist that question is. And yet, switching back to the Korean conference, no one there found this sort of question—in essence the same question as the ones I just described—no one found this odd at all, except for me. And think also of the interesting implications of the second question: if a Korean-American asks if Korean-Americans can blame the Americans for making Koreans racist, then what exactly is going on here? Are Korean-Americans somehow not Americans? Or is this a classic case of the *hyphen-of-convenience*—American when it is something good, but a quick leap across the hyphen to Korean when it is something bad (like racism)? But wait, there's more: what about this whole category of "the Americans" who are allegedly to blame for Korean racism? Perhaps the student is referring to the American troops that have been in South Korea to help protect that country since the Korean war armistice in 1953. Apparently, the Americans came and brought their racism with them. Those US troops have all come from a variety of diverse backgrounds, so on the one hand this could be the ultimate equalizer: Americans in Korea from all different backgrounds are equally racist and equally culpable in making Koreans racist. On the other hand, if the assumption is that in using the phrase "the Americans" the questioner really meant "white Americans," then we have an even bigger mess on our hands. As I discussed earlier, the tendency to assume that non-white people in America are not Americans is itself often cited as an example why America is "so racist," but in this case a non-white, Korean-American person has made the assumption that "Americans" are really white Americans, which would make *her* (the Korean-American student who asked the question) the racist. And since the alleged racism was created by Americans, and since the questioner was Korean-American, and since Korean-Americans are as American as any other American, it would mean that if Americans made Koreans into racists, then the questioner forced herself to be racist against herself. That's quite a trick for diversity to pull off.

Absurdist fun aside, there is a very serious danger in the predilection for involution and the narcissism it creates for the potential that diversity has to shape and create a just and vibrant and integrated society in America. It concerns me, for instance, from both an educational and a social viewpoint, that an American student of Indian descent would take the time to come to my office hours—having never come to my office hours before (or since)—to tell me that I should not say anything bad about India in my lectures because other students might get the "wrong idea" about India. I had given a lecture that discussed the caste system in India in the larger context of systematic inequality around the world, but according to this student, the caste system no longer existed in India and so it wasn't a problem. To put it mildly, her so-called insight was and still is pure idiocy. But the main reason it concerns me is that it is really a request for censorship, a request to restrain the power of the First Amendment so that only good things can be said of other cultures in our classrooms. Remember, the whole justification of diversity in the classroom is to provide the "robust exchange of ideas," and here is yet one more example of how that doesn't happen. It concerns me also because the student has no problem with a critical presentation of America itself, or of any other country or culture I discussed, but India was singled out as a country that could only be praised. It concerns me because the student came to my office hours apparently at the urging of her father (that's what she said), and apparently her father has raised her to believe that India is a veritable paradise of all that is good and perfect in the world, including the delusional and mendacious view that caste and the other outrages in Indian society that ruin the lives of millions of people every day somehow no longer exist.[21] It concerns me because this type of censorship is demanded in the

---

[21] They very much do still exist. See, among many other references, Pawan Dixit, "Living in fear: Dalits still at receiving end of caste atrocities in Uttar Pradesh," *Hindustan Times* (January 31, 2017) at http://www.hindustantimes.com/india-news/living-in-fear-dalits-still-at-receiving-end-of-caste-atrocities-in-uttar-pradesh/story-f8M4EkiPEGeVy6kwadODSP.html

name of diversity, and thus diversity takes the form of someone trying to shove an ignorance-soaked sock down my throat to stifle the creativity of the educational process. Education and diversity should make us see everything that occurs, both among ourselves and among others, and to understand what is collectively good but also what is collectively bad. But when diversity becomes a form of censorship, American democracy begins to wither, and when that happens, everyone loses.

CHAPTER 4

PUTTING CULTURE IN ITS PLACE

Democracy and Diversity

When California voters decided to ban racial preferences by enacting Proposition 209 in 1996, rallies were held at college campuses all around California fighting to repeal or overturn the proposition in order to defend affirmative action. One of those rallies was held at UC Berkeley—of course Berkeley would have a rally—and featured a number of distinguished speakers who were there to address and inspire and mobilize the crowd and to speak about why affirmative action was such an essential part of social justice in California and in the United States. One of the speakers, a professor at the law school, began her speech with the line: "So hey, what are all these white men so scared about?" After a thunderous roar of approval from the audience, the speaker began to explain why affirmative action programs were not a threat to anyone's power. The only thing that affirmative action programs ask for, she explained, is that if you end up in a situation where the two final candidates for a job are equally qualified, then at that point you might—just might—consider the racial or ethnic background of one of the candidates and show a preference. Was it really such a crime to ask that in a situation of equal competence, someone

Understanding the Misunderstanding

from a group who had never been given a chance finally got that chance?

At the time of the rally I was writing my doctoral dissertation and was thus making the transition into the professional marketplace. As a graduate student, and since then as a member of the academic profession, justice has always been the central theme of every research project I have undertaken (including this book). So when someone talks about justice at a rally like this, I take it very seriously and I also give it the respect it is due by thinking through the argument deeply and clearly. I do remember even at the time, in attendance at the rally, feeling uncomfortable with a speaker describing the debate over affirmative action as something white men fear but everyone else wants. It seemed a racially divisive way to advocate a program that was supposed to take us all past racial divisions. I also knew that many of the supporters of the ban on affirmative action and racial preferences were not white and were not men, so apparently they had been discarded as traitors to their "true" identity and had committed the ultimate identity crime of "becoming white." A rather simplistic judicial calculus had been employed—and this from a top-ranked university that should have shown a little more insight and wisdom—that claimed that injustice was white and male, so whatever was not white and not male, or any combination thereof, was automatically a color-coded and pre-packaged form of justice. Any exceptions to this black-or-white rule were discounted and excoriated as sell-outs. For affirmative action to create diversity of identity, it seems, diversity of thought had to be eliminated among its supporters.

One of the things I did not have any experience with at the time was the way that affirmative action programs actually work. The speaker at the rally was right in her explanation as to how affirmative action programs were *supposed* to work. But what I have learned since then, in my subsequent professional career, is that the way the programs are supposed to work, and the way they are actually implemented, are irreconcilably different. In practice, most affirmative action programs do not create justice from injustice, but rather replace one form of injustice with another. The reason for this is that more often than not, decisions about whom to hire are made long before the screening of candidates gets anywhere near the final short list. Although the members of the hiring committee are supposed to consider a racial preference only if there is an equal match in the qualifications of the final candidates, what usually happens is that at the start of the search process, at the very first meeting of the hiring committee, the director of the search committee will announce a target: "we're looking for an Asian female," or "we're searching for someone ethnic" (yes, "ethnic" is code for non-white). The applications are then pre-filtered in that direction. Many institutions, including academic ones, employ affirmative action officers who monitor the hiring process to make sure there is "sufficient" diversity in each department. It is not at all uncommon for the affirmative action officer to weigh in with her or his preferences by making it clear that they will try to veto any choice of candidate that does not match the affirmative action officer's preferences.

I mention all of this to point out that there is a fundamental flaw in the way the debate over affirmative action is framed. To advocate for affirmative action programs by confusing the way that affirmative action law is *written* with the way it is actually *practiced* is a bit like saying that people of color in America have nothing to complain about on the grounds that the Fourteenth Amendment already provides equality before the law. It would be like a parent explaining to the police that her sixteen-year-old daughter who is spewing appletini-scented vomit on her prom dress could not *possibly* be drunk because the legal drinking age is twenty-one. What the law says does not correlate with the sad reality in front of her. Seriously, who thinks this way? Who confuses the text of the law with the palpable reality of how it is practiced? Probably the same kind of person who thinks Spongebob Squarepants is some type of contraceptive device. For something as significant and as contested and as controversial as affirmative action, situated as it is in the larger debate on the role of diversity in American society, there is a breathtaking lack of inspired thought and practical awareness to move any of this tired rhetorical behemoth in the direction of meaningful or substantive justice.

I also mention this for the deleterious effect that this imperfect and truncated debate has on the larger democratic processes in which it is deeply embedded. Part of that negative effect comes from the fact that what should be a hearty and robust democratic debate on the role of racial preferences and affirmative action on the quality of American democracy shows surprisingly little democratic content at all. Once the discussion is distilled down to a simplistic two-choice debate that is voiced in a language that even babies would find confusingly simplistic, we end up with two irreconcilable outcomes: (1) *Liberal view*—either you are a dominant, white male racist or you support fairness and justice through affirmative action, or, (2) *Conservative view*—either you are a proponent of individual rights and rational democracy or you are a welfare-leeching entitlement-loving work-shunning ward of the state. With choices like these, we in effect have no choice. It's like we are having a national debate on whether we should beat our kids more or beat them less, and no one is asking the painfully obvious question of whether we should be beating our kids at all. Isn't there some other possibility we haven't tried yet?

Not everyone who supports affirmative action does so for the most noble of reasons: some people—and I have met them—are not shy about stating that the job market right now is horrible and any advantage you can claim, including "playing the race card," is worth using. Not everyone who opposes affirmative action does so for principled reasons either: some people—and I have met them, too—are not shy about blaming the underclass for everything that is wrong in America, the brake that is holding back the juggernaut that should be the unbridled American economy. But somewhere in between are a lot of people, and they come from a variety of diverse backgrounds, who are simply uncomfortable with the way things are right now in the world of diversity policy and practice, including affirmative action programs. They would like to see change based on ideas rather than on identity-based advocacy movements. If the best we can offer to those individuals is to denounce them as "privileged white men" (if they happen to be one) or as "sell-outs" or "race-traitors" (if they are not white men), then the best we have to offer is really just a stinking load of garbage (and in my profession I see a *lot* of garbage). American democracy deserves better and needs better. American diversity demands it.

All of this raises the question of what the relationship is between democracy and diversity, and perhaps more importantly, what that relationship *should* be. Both democracy and diversity have public elements and private elements, and it is the quality of the connection between the two—public and private—that determines the vibrancy and fluidity of both. In democracy, for instance, we have the public elements of events (such as elections) or persons (such as elected officials) coexisting alongside the private elements of groups (such as civil society organizations), and institutions (such as a free and independent press). There are literally hundreds if not thousands of moving parts to this complex political machine, and getting even one or two out of alignment can compromise the efficiency and effectiveness of the whole thing. Strengthen the public and weaken the private, and you get citizen disempowerment and tyranny. Strengthen the private and weaken the public, and you get an unresponsive state and demagoguery. The cost of failure can be catastrophic, but the payoff of success can be a quality of life that no other political system can even hope to match.

Diversity also has public and private elements, and like democracy, it is imperative that these two different sets of elements create a symbiotic and complementary mode of operation that enhances and reinforces both. The public elements of diversity include various programs and policies, such as affirmative action programs at the local, state, and federal levels, through which the government tries to create a diverse society in accordance with its own model of what a diverse society should be. The private elements of diversity include the actions of individuals and of civil society groups, and can consist of things such as the choice of location to study or work abroad, the choice of language to study or to use, the type of civil organization an individual joins (is it identity-based or issue-based?), and so on. But diversity as a comprehensive project has relied very heavily—too heavily, in my opinion—on public instruments such as courts and public policy in the effort to create a more diversified society. As a result, the private elements of the project, those paths that relate to the civic and civil responsibility of individuals in society, have weakened and atrophied. And when individuals shirk or avoid or evade these responsibilities in a democratic society, the result tends to be an over-reliance on public instruments, and also, in the private sphere, over-reliance on collective rather than individual action. In other words, the failure to embrace the private and individual responsibilities of diversity has created a strong preference for narrow-minded and narcissistic group-think.

Culture and group-think
This preference for group-think is manifested in several different ways. It is represented and also exacerbated, for instance, in the process of identity group involution that I described in the previous chapter. It is also prevalent in the viewpoint that society should somehow have more people that "look like me," a strange and paradoxical preference for sameness in the name of diversity. It can also be seen in the advocacy styles of groups that push for more public policy that promotes diversity: more often than

not, these groups are identity-based groups who are advocating for a greater share of public goods based on their own identity. All of these identity-groups represent a pre-packaged platform of values, based on a pre-packaged identity (one need only embrace one's ethnicity, race, etc. to belong), and the only requirement for group affiliation is to assimilate fully to the pre-packaged values and activities of the group. No real action is involved: membership is effortless, thoughtless, and nearly risk-free. The result is that the public debate over diversity consists primarily of different identity-groups who paradoxically stifle diversity within their ranks to present a unified front *to* society but at the same time demand more diversity *from* society. This is unsustainable and unproductive. It's also ridiculous.

Just as Einstein famously observed that you cannot simultaneously prevent and prepare for war, so too is it impossible to simultaneously promote and prevent diversity. Over and over again, advocates point to the deeply entrenched power of the dominant group—"the enemy" or "the white man"—as the obstacle that prevents diversity from happening, when in fact the greatest obstacle is the anemic strategizing and opaque vision of the advocacy groups themselves. The only way out of this rut—and it is a very, very deep rut—is to craft a new set of policies and to create a new civic space that can eliminate or least mitigate the effects of group-think in the conception and construction of American diversity. And the only way to eliminate and mitigate the effects of group-think is to eliminate or mitigate the influence of the group. And of course the only way to eliminate or mitigate the influence of the group is resuscitate and reconstruct *the role of the individual* in American political life.

Group-think is the death-knell of democracy. It is also the death-knell of diversity. It would be hard to overestimate the climate of fear and the muzzling of expression and creative thought that group-think has produced in the discourse on diversity. Every single time I introduce a discussion of diversity and diversity-related issues in my classes, there is usually an awkward and uncomfortable silence that follows every question I pose. But it's what happens after the class that is the most telling, and in many ways the most hopeful. One by one, what I hear are students who are uncomfortable with the way "their" identity group forces a particular viewpoint on pretty much everything, including diversity, and yet to express this discomfort openly, they have to face the trial-by-fire gamut of their identity-based cohort and risk social ostracism for expressing dissent. Dissent, they are told, weakens the group and therefore ruins the chances of diversity for everyone else in the group. While there are many advocates of current diversity policy who will claim that you "can't argue with results" and will point to various victories whereby certain groups have achieved more visibility in American society, I would posit that this is based on specious reasoning at best. That is, I do not think it is the group-think advocacy for public programs such as affirmative action that has made American society more comfortable with diversity. Rather, it is the more subtle insurrections of spirited individuals who have struggled to move past the identity-as-destiny orthodoxy created through group-think involution that has made the most impressive difference in changing people's minds. In other words, to the extent that there has been any success in diversity over the past two or three decades, diversity has succeeded in spite of public policy, not because of it.

To return to the idea of resuscitating or rescuing the individual from the mind-trap of group-think, it is worth a moment or two to understand exactly what is so important about the individual as a political unit and the crucial role that individualism plays in constructing a vibrant democracy. The first point to clarify is that "Western individualism" is one of the most misunderstood concepts we have in political theory and cultural studies. Cultural psychologists are fond of belching out volumes of infantile prattle about how the world is divided up into what are either individualized cultures or communal cultures, but the truth is never as binary or as tidy as that. Other critics like to point out that Western individualism is really a myth, that even Western cultures rely heavily on larger collective social networks for both security and opportunity. In reality, that insight is about as useful as the observation that water is wet. *Of course* Western individualism is a myth, to the extent it embodies the idea that every Westerner negotiates the complexities of life on her or his own without any help from anyone. But so too is the non-Western traditional extended family a myth, to the extent that it embodies the idea that every non-Western family lives in a harmonious multi-generational household fighting only over who should make the greatest sacrifice for the others. There is just as much human misery and suffering in Western families that fall apart due to the selfish individualism of one member as there is in non-Western families that are kept together for no other reason than tradition said it had to be so. Culture can generate comfort and dysfunction with equal ease pretty much anywhere that culture exists, which is everywhere.

The second point to make here is to specify what the substantive elements of individualism are. Contrary to popular belief or urban legend, individualism in the context of democracy should never be construed to mean selfish or egotistical behavior. Yes, there are plenty of economists who will tell you otherwise, who will tell you that the marketplace is all about maximizing one's self-interest, and that one's self-interest should not be limited by the state or any other external agent. Many of those economists like to quote Adam Smith on this point, but show me an economist who attributes this line of thinking to Adam Smith and I'll show you an economist who is a flagrant idiot. Adam Smith was a moral philosopher first, always first, and an economist only a distant second at best. The reason that Smith championed the free market was not to celebrate the unbridled self-interest of the individual, but rather to allow a free space, simultaneously public and private, in which individuals could try out different preferences in a continuous dress rehearsal of ethics and morality, and do so—and here is the important part—in concert with other individuals engaged in the same individualist project. The marketplace was to be a forum in which individuals could work out their own civic preferences, freed from the directives of the state, and freed from the constraints of communal institutions. Collectively—as a collection of individuals—they would work out the optimal arrangement of preferences in terms of available goods, fair prices, fair practices, and so forth. If the state ever got involved in the market, it was only to be a temporary fix, and only as a gentle corrective when things had gone in a direction that undermined the primary purpose of the market (such as with the formation of monopolies).

The link between the economics of Smith's marketplace and the politics of democracy is that the forum of democracy is supposed to work in the same manner, only with our preferences being political rather than economic, and the marketplace being more one of ideas rather than goods. As actors in the democratic marketplace, we enter a forum that is simultaneously public and private, and we determine our optimal preferences in concert with others in the marketplace, who expose us to their ideas and preferences as we expose them to ours. In the best and most vibrant of democracies, the actors in the democratic market place—collectively known as "civil society"—ensure as much individual freedom as possible so that these actors may explore any and all varieties of thought and action in making the determination as to which is the optimal pathway to choose. Note that once again, this is not egotistical selfishness in action. Because our preferences are determined in concert with other individuals, we learn that our own preferences are not the only possible preferences that can be made. Aside from developing our own preferences, we also are supposed to learn social ethics—what used to be called "civics"—in ways that challenge us to find the right balance between what is good for ourselves (self-interest) and what is good for others (empathy). The fewer the constraints placed upon this process, the better the quality of democracy we create.

The potato chip theory of democracy and diversity
So where does diversity fit into all of this? Though he never would have used the word, diversity was very much present in the moral thought of Adam Smith. After all, the only way to determine if one's preferences are optimal is to compare them with all other preferences available, which means having the requisite freedom and open access to explore all other options available in the course of making and articulating one's chosen preferences. The broader the array of ideas and goods we can be exposed to—that is, the greater the diversity of those ideas and goods—the better and more efficient is the marketplace, whether it is the marketplace of goods or ideas. This is the "robust exchange of ideas" referenced in the *Grutter* decision in relation to diversity (the same one, as I have pointed out, that never actually happens). The same holds true for the democratic process: the only way to determine if our voting preferences and choices are optimal is to compare them to all other available choices, which means we need to explore those other available choices, and also weigh our personal preferences and choices in terms of what is good for ourselves versus what is good for others. Just as we need to be prepared to admit that other ideas we explore may be preferable and superior to our own and to alter our preferences accordingly, so too must we also be prepared to admit that the needs of others sometimes outweigh the needs of ourselves, and be prepared to alter out preferences accordingly. In the context of our current democracy in the United States, diversity is supposed to broaden our menu of choices, and as participants in the democratic process, it becomes our civic duty—for *all of us* and not just for those in the majority group—to explore all of the

new ideas that emerge as a result of new entrants and participants bringing new ideas into the democratic forum. Indeed, failure to seek out, learn about, and explore those options amounts to a failure of our civic duty and a distortion of the democratic process.

As an illustrative example of all of this, I present the potato chip theory of everything. Consider the market in potato chips (also known as "crisps" in some other parts of the world, but in those parts of the world people also drive on the wrong side of the road, so in the interest of public safety, please refer to them as chips). In a tightly regulated or constrained market, the availability of choices will be artificially restricted. In a fascist market, for instance, the government will make the choice for you and your role will be either to like the fascist chip or to like prison (and your prison meal will no doubt consist of fascist chips). In a communist market, on the other hand, the existence of multiple choices will be branded as elitist and bourgeois, and so in the name of the revolution, the proletariat chip will be offered, tasteless and rarely available but ideologically delicious. Plus each bag comes with a plastic sickle-and-hammer inside, or perhaps a get-out-of-the-gulag-free card. In a democratic market, however, the choice of potato chip brands and flavors will be seemingly endless, and intentionally so, in order to allow the widest diversity of choices possible so that we can rest assured our final choice of chip will be the optimal choice. Granted it comes with a few drawbacks. Go to any supermarket in America on pretty much any day and you will find at least one person staring at the wall of potato chip options with the same blank stare of stupefaction with which people look at assembly instructions for pretty much any product from IKEA. The potato chip aisle can be intimidating, but our civic duty and our party dignity (as in, our ability to host a good party, even if it's a communist party) require us to make an informed choice, and so we develop a strategy for choosing the best chip possible. Sometimes we develop a trust in certain brands, sometimes we develop a taste for specific flavors, and sometimes we live on the edge and go for the unorthodox choice—durian-flavored chips, anyone?—and often we live with the shame and regret of our poorly-informed choice for days or weeks afterward.

Still, the poorest choices are often the most valuable since it is from them that we learn from our mistakes. Although cynics will often decry the whole process as an excuse to turn us into consumers in the capitalist market, it is worthwhile to remember that we do not need to purchase every available brand of potato chips on earth to make an informed choice. We can always ask for the insights of others whose choices we respect, or do our own online research to seek the opinion of chip experts, if such a profession exists. If we embrace our chip duties seriously, eventually inferior and undesirable flavors and brands will fall out of the market and our collective preferences will leave a broad array of only the most optimal choices in the marketplace.

So, having explored the potato chip theory of democracy and the pivotal role of the individual in developing preferences in the public and private spheres, what conclusion does this offer us about the current state of diversity and its relationship to the quality of democracy in America? One of the worst by-products and trends of the combination of diversity and democracy has been the growing tendency to create identity-based voting blocs that go by such labels as "the Asian vote" or "the Hispanic vote" and so on (for some reason we don't have "the women's vote" but we do have "women voters"). I call them one of the worst by-products because they are often seen as a *positive* development, a new assertiveness by formerly marginalized groups who are using a strength-in-numbers approach to amplify their voting power in American democracy and using collective voting preferences as a path to move away from the margins and toward the center. And yet, for the very reasons I just explained in considerable detail, the cost of this trend to American democracy in the long run is unacceptably high. The

Understanding the Misunderstanding

reason for this is quite simple: creating collective, identity-based vote-blocs undermines the type of critical thinking at the individual level that is absolutely essential for the vibrancy and the fairness of *any* democracy, including American democracy. The substitution of pre-packaged voting preferences based on the presumed collective interests of a particular identity group also brings us back to a similar problem that I discussed earlier: the only way to articulate "the Hispanic vote" is to ask Hispanics to assimilate to a homogeneous Hispanic mindset, and thus a vote that appears to be engaged with democracy through diversity on the outside only exists if diversity is denied on the inside. If diversity were working properly, the way it was designed to work, there would be no "Hispanic vote" and no "Asian vote" or any other such group-think vote.

If diversity exists in order to expose us to as many different ideas as possible, and to learn from them and to learn from others to better understand ourselves, then the whole electoral project of creating and defining an ethnic vote, a pre-packaged set of normative preferences to articulate what a person from a particular identity group should think and want (politically speaking) is not diversity at all but rather the antithesis of diversity. For an Asian-American to imbibe "the Asian vote" or for a Hispanic to do the same with "the Hispanic vote" is like walking into a grocery store and buying "the Asian chip" or "the Hispanic chip" without ever trying any other flavor and without ever questioning the advice of the person who told you that was the best and only flavor for you. Voting primarily along ethnic lines is akin to a distortion of the democratic market, a sort of ethnic monopoly that compromises the integrity of the marketplace of ideas. The problem with a monopoly, in the thinking of Adam Smith and other theorists of the democratic market, is that it frees the monopolist from having to consider the interests of others and reduces competition to the point where the monopolist thinks only of what is best for her or his monopoly, rather than what is best for the market. This is why in Adam Smith's philosophy of the marketplace, monopolies were one of the few situations in which the government should intervene, in order to break up the monopoly (which is economically narcissistic) and restore the open market. If we apply that lesson to the democratic marketplace of ideas, it means that government intervention in favor of diversity should be in favor of breaking down ethnic voting blocs rather than courting them, and that is as true for majority groups as it is for minority ones.

Imagine, for instance, walking into a grocery store to find each aisle labeled "the Asian aisle" or "the Latino aisle" or "the White aisle," and so on. Suppose each of those aisles comes pre-stocked with all the food preferences that a person from that identity group is supposed to have, as determined by the "identity managers" (aka, "community leaders") for each aisle. Now suppose when you walk into that store, before you get a chance to look around too much, clerks at the entrance try to figure out which aisle fits your profile and quickly escort you to the appropriate aisle: "Here you go, Mr. Asian, everything you need and want will be found right here on the Asian aisle. The decision has already been made for you—you don't even have to think. And indeed, we hope you don't." I would like to think that even if I whiled away the afternoon by repeatedly shooting a nail gun directly into my own brain, at the end of the day I would still be able to see that as one creepy and dysfunctional and racist grocery store. And yet, that grocery store is not too far off the mark in describing the gist of identity-based political mobilization in contemporary America. And what is more, by our current, abysmally-skewed standards, that grocery store would be called "diverse."

So, how should we rearrange that grocery store, to make it more diverse in a better, more constructive way? For starters, having different aisles of preferences is not the problem, so this is not a question of structure. The problem is with the customers and the consumers, who for some reason have allowed themselves to be shown a particular aisle and have embraced the security and comfort of all that is familiar and all that is similar in that aisle. That set-up can only be called diverse by the emptiest of minds. What you need and want in a situation like this is for one person, and then another, to *leave* their aisle to see what other people on other aisles are doing, what they are choosing, what they are eating, what different tastes they have. Once one or two people leave their aisles, others will follow, and then still others, and soon we will have a very different experience at our local Diversity Mart: Asians will shop on the African aisle, Africans will shop on the Latino aisle, Latinos will shop on the White aisle, everyone will be shopping on all the different aisles. Whole new conversations will spring up: "I had no idea our preferences were so similar, though we come from different backgrounds," or "What is this ingredient and how do you use it?" or "I thought only Asians could make this dish, but it looks like anyone can!" And that, in a nutshell, is what diversity should look like and sound like. Note the paradoxical lesson that is learned from this: diversity works best when people walk *away* from their group, not when people walk *toward* their group.

Why culture is not resistance
If the door to the magical land of diversity were locked with several locks of different shapes and sizes (even the locks would be diverse, of course), this simple and simply revolutionary act of walking away would be the first key that opens one or perhaps even more than one of those locks. So why then do so few people actually do it? Why is the trend instead to seek out homogeneous and non-diverse groups of people who "look like me"? There are many excuses and objections often made for this, and here I will take up a few and show why they should not and cannot be accepted.

Objection #1: Assimilation to the values of the group strengthens those values and gives people in the group a sense of belonging. If people resist assimilation within the group and walk away to interact with other cultures, the group will fall apart and the identity will be destroyed.

One of the odd things about this oft-repeated objection is that it contains a deliciously unresolved contradiction: if diversity within a group breaks the group apart, then wouldn't diversity in America break America apart? This objection seems to imply that the best policy approach for the United States to follow would be to dismantle all diversity-related programs and then begin an aggressive assimilation campaign, in order to prevent America from falling apart through the expression of difference. If that seems like a scary thought for America, it should seem like a scary thought anywhere it exists. No one said that walking away from a group identity had to be a complete break or a rejection of that identity. But moving ourselves out of our own group and into the company of others does modify and diversify our sense of self. It shows us that there are many different ways to be Latino, and many different ways to be Armenian, and so on, just as there are many different ways to be American. Just because there are a million ways to be American does not mean that America ceases to exist. Indeed, the freedom to be what you want to be is the most eloquent expression of America that we have. It should also be the most eloquent expression of diversity within any group. All too often, what we call "community building" in identity-based groups is really just a form of suppressing and stifling diversity from within.

Objection #2: Identity-based groups, especially for minority groups, are effective ways to develop and express the preferences of the group to ensure proper representation in the political process.

First things first: in a non-diverse and homogeneous social environment, where the group moves in unison, preferences are not *developed,* they are *enforced.* This is what makes joining these types of groups, and accepting their expression of identity, so easy: no thinking is required. They offer a pre-packaged, pre-conceived list of preferences, and a pre-fabricated social community, and the price of admission is acceptance of those preferences, which is ironically the textbook definition of assimilation. The individual in essence disappears into the collective. It is unclear to me how this helps contribute anything to democracy or to the political process. Much of my heritage, for instance, is Swiss-German. I suppose I could express my ethnic heritage in some visible way, perhaps by smearing Ricola-scented chocolate fondue all over my body while I yodel in my lederhosen (which might actually be a thing among hipsters), but while I am quite certain that it would make for an interesting spectacle, I am less certain about how it would give me clarity and insight in developing my political preferences or casting my vote in elections. Adopting and following the pre-packaged preferences of an identity-based group is a bit like me giving an examination and providing each student with the answers while they take the exam. The students will all do well and feel a great sense of accomplishment, since they all will get an A on the exam, but in reality, aside from good feelings and a boost in personal self-esteem, nothing else has been accomplished and no one has learned a thing. It gives the illusion of learning without any real substance. Learning, like diversity, has to have substance.

The second problem with this objection is that it concentrates on the wrong political unit: in democracies, *individuals* are represented, not groups. That is why we vote as individuals. True, there are political parties, but people join or follow political parties by matching their personal preferences to a party platform, which makes them collectives of individuals who have made similar choices. This is a fundamental difference from pre-packaged identity-based groups, where the individual merely imbibes and embraces pre-existing group preferences. Alternatively put, political parties represent individuals who have *made* similar choices, but identity-based groups represent individuals who want to *avoid* making choices. Membership is also different: political parties are inclusive (anyone can join), whereas identity-based groups are exclusive (only persons with that identity can join). *What this means in practice is that in the political process, identity-based groups represent exclusive voting blocs whose collective vote is based on a preference for whichever political party will deliver the greatest benefits to members of that group.* Note that the focus is narrowly on one's own group, and not on the needs of other groups, other individuals, or the country as a whole. To ask the question, "which party gives more money for and support to affirmative action?" and then to vote for that party because your group benefits from those policies is a very different approach than asking the question, "is affirmative action really the best way to achieve diversity?" and then to weigh the consequences not just for your own group, but for other groups and for the whole national project of diversity. Group-based preferences become in essence political versions of class-action law suits, filed through elections rather than through the courts, to demand a greater share of political resources from the state, based on the idea that the needs and wants of the group are uniformly consistent and non-diverse. For both diversity and democracy, this practice is strangely non-diverse and unsettlingly undemocratic.

Objection #3: Identity-based groups must reflect a unified and homogeneous viewpoint in order to resist the attempts of the dominant group to dismantle all opposing identities and their cultures. The reason that diversity cannot be tolerated within minority groups, and the reason that walking away is not an option, is because it renders the entire group vulnerable to oppression by the dominant group.

This is obviously the most contentious of the objections, based as it is on the assumption that the dominant group in a society is not just numerically dominant but actively and intentionally oppressive in exerting and protecting its dominance. Minority groups are assumed to be always and everywhere oppressed in this scenario, and the only way for them to fight back is to band together and create a unified front. Individuals in these minority groups who want to go their own way or find a different way to articulate their identity are therefore either threats to the others in the group or active collaborators with the oppressors. The call for individuals to "think for themselves" is seen as an attempt by the majority group to lure individuals away from minority groups, to make these individuals more vulnerable and exposed and to weaken the threat from minority groups by weakening their unity. In other words, the exhortation for citizens to think for themselves is really just a big plot to allow more oppression to occur.

There are multiple problems with this objection. The most obvious one is that it does not require and sometimes cannot prove any direct and intentional oppression: there is an assumption that majority groups will always oppress and smaller groups will always be oppressed. Oppression is somehow just "there"—always. The power dynamic in this scenario stretches only from the majority group to all other groups. No oppressive links between or within the other groups are explored or considered, and this is the fundamental blind spot of this approach. If majority groups oppress because they are larger than other groups, then it also follows that any group that is larger than any other group will oppress that group as well. Minority-to-minority oppression is equally prevalent, as is oppression within minority groups, but these are expressly left out of the equation, giving us only a simplified and distorted view of how social forces really work. This is why so many minority groups see no contradiction in advocating for more inclusiveness and diversity in society, in order to counteract the oppression of the majority group, but then deny the same thing for sub-groups within the minority group (such as women), when they ask for a similar inclusiveness and diversity within the group. *Minorities within minority societies are often far more disempowered than minorities within majority societies.* It seems a basic rule of ethics that you cannot ask for something from one group if you are not also willing to give it to another.

The annoying convenience of cultural relativism
There is another, perhaps more fundamental objection that is often voiced in reaction to the preferential role of the individual in determining the various preferences of the marketplace or the democratic forum. This objection is articulated as a form of irreconcilable cultural difference, and goes something like this: if my culture values the family or the community more than the individual, then the request or demand that I act and think as an individual is really a request or a demand to dismantle my culture, or at least to alienate me from my cultural environment. If diversity is also a platform for preserving and celebrating the various cultures that exist in America, then this objection would argue that cultures that do not value the individual as much as other social groups have a right to continue to exist as they are, free from any pressure to change, and that it is individualized democracy that should adapt to the different ways of those cultures and not the other way around. Since individualism is a Western trait, at least according to this line of opposition, the request for non-individualist cultures to assimilate to an individualized social framework is really a form of forced assimilation to "Western" values, or Westernized hegemony, or cultural genocide, and so on. At the very least, it is anti-diversity. For these critics, diversity means never having to change.

To a certain extent, this will sound like another variant of the anti-assimilationist position described earlier, but in fact it is something separate and thus requires separate treatment not only because of its obfuscating complexity but also because it shows up frequently outside of American politics in the international arena. It therefore cannot be sidestepped but rather must be engaged.

The first step toward engaging this issue is to pare it down to its essence: what exactly is being claimed here? The claim consists of a number of elements that need to be considered separately, though they are all simultaneously present. These elements are: (1) that culture is tangible and exists in a uniformly consistent manner within clearly-demarcated cultural boundaries; (2) that culture does not change over time and so is static rather than dynamic; (3) that culture cannot and should not mix with or absorb values outside of itself; (4) that culture is an absolute value that cannot be questioned or judged. The short response to these individual elements, as I shall show in more detail momentarily, is that none of them is true. But there is a second part to this claim that needs to be considered as well. In essence, this is a claim of cultural relativism, one of the most vexing and intractable forms of argument that has a frustrating ability to shut down nearly any discussion in which it rears its convoluted head. Here we cannot rely on any counter-argument to show whether cultural relativism is true or false, since it is not that kind of conceptual beast. Instead, we have to employ a different approach, and that is the approach of shifting the perspective to something besides culture. In short, I will show that this objection, though couched in terms of culture and cultural relativism, is really a question of *ethical* principles rather than one of cultural norms.

It is important not to underestimate the significance and the challenge of this line of argument and this point of view, however insubstantial it may first appear. In the world of human rights, for instance, which happens to be one of the fields in which I work, the cultural relativist argument is often invoked by many countries to avoid scrutiny of human rights violations by claiming that human rights are really "Western values" that cannot and should not be applied to non-Western countries. One relatively recent example of this would be the Pussy Riot brouhaha that took place in Russia in August 2012, in which an alternative all-female music group named Pussy Riot staged a protest event at a church by playing a song mocking Russian president Vladimir Putin, an act for which they were put on trial and then sentenced to two years in prison for the crime of "hooliganism." In the international outcry that ensued, mostly against the harshness of the sentence and the growing crack-down on freedom of speech and political protest in putatively-democratic Russia, the official response from the Russian administration was that there was no room and no place for "Western values" or "Western rights" in Russian culture.[22] Of course, which specific aspects of Russian culture were irreconcilable with human rights were never detailed. Russian culture was simply invoked as a non-Western blanket to shield the Russian government from any outside criticism.

Similarly, in China, where growing disenchantment over corruption and one-party rule has fueled continuous mobilization of citizen-based movements for more democratic forms of politics, the former president of China, Hu Jintao, made it absolutely clear that he believed these movements were part of a larger plot to destroy Chinese culture through the infiltration of "Western-style values." This infiltration had occurred either as a result of foreign agents themselves or as a result of Chinese citizens who had "erroneously" imbibed the cultural values of non-Chinese cultures. President Hu warned of these dangers, particularly of the danger of China being split apart by the presence and influence of these culturally inappropriate and foreign (read Western) values, in an address to the leaders of the Chinese Communist Party in October 2011.[23] In a classic "what's-wrong-with-this-picture" type

---

22 For a more detailed account, see Jeanne Park, "Putin's Culture War," *The Atlantic* (August 20, 2012) at https://www.theatlantic.com/international/archive/2012/08/putins-culture-war/261318/

23 See Michael Bristow, "China rules out West's democracy," *BBC News* (October 15, 2007) at http://news.bbc.co.uk/2/hi/asia-pacific/7043942.stm

of scenario, here we have the president of China addressing the leaders of the ruling Communist Party in China about the dangers of allowing Western ideas and ideologies into China, and yet no one present, neither speaker nor audience, perceives or admits the irony that the ideology of the entire ruling apparatus of China—socialism—is itself a Western ideology.[24] (On a side note, since socialism is the transitional ideology that oversees the revolutionary process which culminates in the attainment of pure communism, both socialism and communism are as Western in their pedigrees as democracy.) True, one could argue that Maoism is a distinctly Chinese variant of Marxist socialist thought (in which the rural peasant rather than the urban worker becomes the key catalyst of revolutionary action), but the ruling party in China is the Chinese Communist Party, not the Chinese Maoist Party. Besides, Maoism has been severely discredited in China since the economic reforms begun by Deng Xiaoping back in the late 1970s and early 1980s. *The point here is to notice that an objection phrased in terms of culture is not really about culture at all; it is about power.* What Hu Jintao is really saying is that Western ideologies (socialism and communism) that entrench and enrich the dominance of the ruling party are fine, but Western ideologies that encourage Chinese citizens to think for themselves and hence see through and question the propaganda that is force-fed to them through government-controlled media are "inappropriate" and "unacceptable" and of course "foreign."

On a side note, I will point out with none too little irony that Maoism is a reconciliation of a Western ideological line of thought (Leninism via Marxism to produce socialism, which leads to communism) with the reality of Chinese society at the time, which was

---

24 See Chan Kai Yee, "China says western-style democracy impossible for CCP dynasty," *China Daily Mail* (March 13, 2013) at https://chinadailymail.com/2013/03/13/china-says-western-style-democracy-impossible-for-ccp-dynasty/

largely rural and thus peasant-based. What that means is that if the claims of China's leadership, based on the concept of cultural relativism, that foreign ideas are inappropriate for China, then Maoism as an ideology is both an inherent contradiction and an absolute impossibility. This would make the entire edifice and essence of contemporary China—remember, it was Mao himself who was the chief architect, politically and ideologically, of the People's Republic of China—bankrupt and invalid. The only way to save Maoism and save the essence of the Chinese state is therefore to admit that foreign ideas can easily be incorporated into Chinese polity and society. In other words, it would be just as easy and just as culturally appropriate for China to become democratic as it would to become socialist. Which it did.

There is another entirely separate way to dismantle the cultural relativist argument embedded in the objection raised by Hu Jintao. One of the other criticisms often levied against "Western" ideologies in China is that in promoting the role of the individual over the family or the group, they undermine Chinese cultural norms that promote the family and group over the individual. Thus, importing Western ideas and Western ways is not just the death-knell of the rule of the Communist Party, it is the death-knell of Chinese culture in general. But what ideology elevated the family to such a prominent level in Chinese culture in the first place? The single most important ideology on that front would be Confucianism, named after its most eloquent proponent, Confucius (from the Mandarin *Kǒng Fū Zǐ*). Two of the most important things about Confucianism that make this an awkward fit at best are that (1) morality and ethics must be learned from direct social circulation, so the heavy-handed socialist state under the control of the Communist Party would have to be dismantled, and (2) the most immoral occupation in existence and the one with the lowest status in Confucianism is that of the merchant, so the expansion of the Chinese economy that has so enriched the Communist

Party and those linked to it in China would also have to be reversed. It is also worthwhile to remember that during the years of the Cultural Revolution in China, Confucius and Confucianism were repeatedly attacked as "reactionary" and backward vestiges of the Chinese past. Even by the standards of Chinese culture, the Chinese Communist Party has already done enough dismantling of Chinese culture whenever it was deemed necessary to deepen its control, so the introduction of democratic values can hardly be a cultural threat. Indeed, according to scholar Tu Weiming, the ideas and principles of Confucianism, when they are allowed to work as they were originally designed, are more inclined to lead to a result that resembles Western democracy, and not socialism or communism. The pro-democracy activists in China might be the most culturally authentic political actors that China has."[25]

Returning to America
So, after this brief detour to Russia and China, what then happens when we bring this idea of cultural relativism back to America to see what it does for the prospects of diversity? In the American context, the objection takes on a variety of forms, just as it does in the international arena, but the intent is quite different. In the American context, the intent is not for instance to stay in power or to cover up human rights abuses, but rather to avoid certain obligations or responsibilities in the mutually shared task of creating and maintaining a diverse society. In simpler language, it means that cultural relativism is often invoked as a justification to avoid assimilation and direct participation in American society (remember, even according to the Supreme Court, the end goal of diversity is an integrated American society). If we accept the current definition of diversity—that it consists simply of the simultaneous

---

[25] See most importantly Tu Weiming, *Humanity and Self-Cultivation: Essays in Confucian Thought* (1999)

existence of different and discrete groups in a shared space, with each group free to practice and maintain its own cultural values and practices—then an expectation for minority groups to assimilate to mainstream values, particularly if those mainstream values are at odds with some of the practices and values of minority groups, is therefore an unfair and discriminatory expectation. There are many reasons to reject this approach to diversity, but for now, let us accept it for what it is and see if the cultural relativist argument maintains legitimacy under closer scrutiny.

At the colloquial level, one of the phrases I often hear from individuals who consider their group identity to be the most important aspect of who they are, and who reject any pressure for assimilation, is some variant of this: *in my culture, family is important*. Whatever variant of this phrasing is used, the point is clear: the speaker is positing that "mainstream American values" are individualistic, and is thus differentiating him or herself from those values by claiming that in a family-centric or group-centric culture, those values must be kept separate from and protected against mainstream American values. There is a second, implicit element of the claim as well, which is that the speaker is also asking to be recognized as fully American, even without fully integrating into American society. It is as if to say: I want to be accepted as a part of American society, but I also want to be apart from American society—I want you to include me, even as I exclude myself. The question that arises is not whether these two elements are reconcilable, but rather whether this position is ethically defensible. My answer is that it is not, and I will now show why.

First, consider the original premise: *in my culture, family is important*. Now consider the hidden premise upon which the statement is based. It is based upon the idea that mainstream American society, or more bluntly, white Western society, is not just individualistic but selfishly so, to the point where Americans relish their ability to neglect their families. There is a certain offensiveness embedded in the claim that implies that somehow, non-Western communities in the United States, or "communities of color," have beautiful and loving values that honor the family, while Westernized and white communities devalue and dishonor their own families and engage in pure, self-indulgent hedonism at the expense of their parents and siblings. The idea that all I do, being of some sort of Westernized lineage, is think of ways to neglect my family and exploit them for my personal needs while sitting in a tattoo parlor getting "I h8 kids" tattooed across the knuckles of my hands, is grotesquely inaccurate and offensive. All cultures value family.

Indeed, I don't know of any community, of any particular color, that doesn't value family and doesn't value them equally as much as any other. I know plenty of people from communities that *claim* to value family more, but in unguarded moments they will speak of the sheer misery that family obligations often create, or they will admit that their community is just as selfish and hedonistic as any other, but their cultural values mandate that such things be covered up and censored out. In the world of culture, there can be no airing of dirty laundry, unless of course it is some other culture's dirty laundry. So the idea that some communities value family more than others is not a valid premise for the resultant action that separates the group from mainstream society and allows them to circulate only among themselves, rather than with other individuals and other groups.

There is another area where individuals from various communities often invoke the idea that they "value family" more than others, and that is when it comes to the issue of marriage. While no one likes to talk openly about it, there are many communities who go to great lengths to insure that their families find a "suitable match" for their children when it comes time for marriage. More specifically, many of these communities do not want their children (especially daughters) dating or even considering the possibility of interacting with others outside of their specific community. I have had many students tell me that their parents have told them, and in some cases forced them, to join an identity-based student group on campus in the hopes that it would limit if not preclude interactions with other people outside the community, out of fear that they might meet and then—horror of horrors—become romantically interested in an "outsider" to the community. I have met parents from a number from many different communities who talk quite strongly about this. At a social event in northern California, for instance, I met a woman from India who was very concerned because her daughter, who was born and raised in America, had started dating a white, Christian boy. She explained that she had taken such efforts to raise her daughter as a "proper Hindu girl," and was now afraid that it was only a matter of time before the boy converted her to Christianity and she would be "lost forever." In the course of the conversation, it became clear that the boy was not a missionary of any sort, and there had been no attempts or even discussion of conversion, but the mother felt quite strongly that it would be only a "matter of time" before it happened. In a similar vein, I can't say how many times I have heard from my Chinese-American students that their parents have given them intense pressure to date other Chinese-Americans because dating an outsider would "dishonor" the family. If it is a dishonor to the family for their children to interact with and date outsiders, then that is not evidence of a strong culture—it is evidence of a racist culture. No one should be protecting that.

Marriage and other romantic relationships are one of the most significant areas where racism in America rears its ugly head yet again. We don't see it, or don't want to see it, because so many groups and persons disguise it as something other than what it is: as "culture" or "family" or some other sort of nonsense. But wrapping racism in the sugary coating of preserving cultural values doesn't make the racism any more palatable or acceptable. A good friend of mine from Indonesia married a white American man:

at nearly every social gathering where Indonesians are present, whether in American or Indonesia, she has to endure the endless comments such as, "So many good men are available in Indonesia, why do you have to choose a foreigner?" That's not Indonesian cultural pride, that's Indonesian racism. I could scroll through example after example from pretty much any cultural group in the United States, showing the true diversity of racism in America, but I would only be filling up pages to make the same point that I have already made. I understand that people from the same identity group can fall in love for reasons that have nothing to do with group identity. I get that. But I also understand how much energy is exerted by so many groups to make sure that each generation "sticks with their own kind." And any time you hear that phrase, no matter who says it, I can guarantee you that the fetid stench of racism is lingering in the air.

Culture is a funny and deadly serious thing
One thing I have never understood is how so many people justify this strain of racism by arguing that marrying outside of one's own group creates a *loss* of culture. Part of this argument rests on the silly assumption that having culture is like having kumquats: something you can measure by the pound. Is there anyone seriously obtuse enough to say, upon hearing that a Latino man married a Korean woman, that between them they "lost" culture? If so, then where did it go, and how much was lost? In fact, since we are talking about diversity in all of this, and since diversity is about celebrating culture, shouldn't we see the marriage of people from different groups as a *gain* of culture, as something that gives us two things where before we had only one, something that gives us twice as much culture as we had before? If culture is a good thing, and the marriage of people from different cultures gives us more of it, shouldn't this be the most valued of unions? I have a good friend in California, for instance, who is a Jewish-American man

married to a Christian woman originally from India. Does their household seethe with identity-based confusion and a diminished sense of cultural perception and experience? Not at all—in fact it is quite the opposite. American, Indian, Jewish and Christian holidays and traditions intermingle seamlessly in a multilingual atmosphere where Sanskrit and Telugu are as likely to be heard as Hebrew and English. What is more important to understand in this context is that the result has not been cultural confusion: no one has ever been concerned that they have been "less American" or "more Indian" or less or more of anything. People who fear that intermingling with other cultures will create identity-based confusion or will compromise their cultural beliefs are usually already confused or compromised to begin with, and more than likely are both.

To bring the discussion back to how the practice of marriage in America reveals the racism associated with maintaining rigid boundaries between different groups—all groups being equally culpable—we can take a closer look at a piece of what is now American pop culture but was once a cutting-edge cinematographic gem of social commentary: the film *Guess Who's Coming to Dinner* (1967). In the original film, the social commentary flows directly from the premise of the film, in which the daughter of a white, upper-class family brings her fiancé home for dinner to meet her parents, and her parents are shocked to discover that her fiancé is black. Part of the shock is produced by the sense of incongruity in what the parents knew about the fiancé before they met him—namely, that his personal and professional credentials were impeccable—versus what they know after they have met him—namely, that he is black. The film is often read as a form of incisive social critique against *white* prejudice and hypocrisy (particularly white liberal prejudice and hypocrisy, since the parents in the film are portrayed as ideologically liberal), but it is far more effectively read as a critique against *any* type of prejudice and hypocrisy.

The premise of the film was partly revamped to make the less insightful but surprisingly still interesting film *Guess Who* in 2005, in which the roles are reversed and the daughter of a black family brings home her less-than-successful white boyfriend. Granted, in the latter film the goal was more comedy than commentary—Ashton Kutcher as the white boyfriend was never in any dramatic competition with Sidney Poitier, the black boyfriend in the original film—but there is one thing about these two films that supports reading the original as a general commentary on all forms of prejudice and hypocrisy rather than a specific commentary on white prejudice and hypocrisy. Although the contexts are reversed in each film, the tension and discomfort that are produced by the proximity of two different groups that normally coexist in different spheres, by the breaching of invisible and sometimes visible social walls between diverse social groups, is equally palpable. The fact is, one could make a version of *Guess Who's Coming to Dinner* for every single community that creates the dazzling diversity of America—majority or minority, and of every religion, race, ethnicity, and culture—and the end result would be exactly the same. In many cases, the outcome would be worse. I cannot emphasize the point enough that anyone who thinks that racism in America is any less diverse than America itself is engaging in a futile exercise of self-delusion that will contribute almost nothing or absolutely nothing to create a platform of diversity that works in any meaningful or useful way.

Now at this point, I can guess that a fair number of readers will be sifting through their ideological damage repair kits to look for justifications or rationalizations for the way things are: the trauma of diaspora, the inculcation of imperialist racism on colonized subjects (more on which later), the difficulty of being a person of color in a white racist society, and so on. But if that is your first reaction, then my succinct response is: please don't. Really, just don't. Anyone who tries to find justifications for this or any other similar commentary from so-called non-dominant communities is doing a tremendous disservice to the ideals of social justice that diversity is supposed to evoke. When a father in America tells his daughter, for instance, not to date a black man, does the identity of the father really matter? If he's a white father, we do not hesitate to call it racism, and it is—the kind of racism that should make any decent human being vomit with disgust and outrage. But if the father is Filipino, or Vietnamese, or Korean—and I can name personal examples of each of those—why do we stumble and hesitate? Why do we want to concoct excuses, rather than call it all out for the racism that it is? If a Filipino father says something like this to his daughter, he is not the victim or product of some larger set of social and historical forces over which he has no control. If he is the victim of anything, it is of his own ignorance, stupidity, and racism. If he's been in America even one day, he has lived here long enough to reflect on this, and the choice he made—to fill his mind with racism and hatred—is entirely his own.

In more tragic cases, parents have even killed their own children rather than let them interact with community outsiders. In January 2008, for instance, Amina and Sarah Said, two teenage Muslim girls who had grown up in America, were shot to death by their own father in Dallas, Texas, allegedly because he discovered that they had shown interest in non-Muslim boys. Elsewhere, in Sweden, Fadime Sahindal, the daughter of Kurdish immigrants, was murdered by her own father, and again for the same reason: Fadime had dared to show interest in a man outside of the Kurdish-Muslim community.[26] These are just two examples of the lengths to which some communities will go to "protect" their culture. And

---

26 On Fadime's story, see Johanne Hildebrandt, "'Honour' killing in Sweden silences courageous voice on ethnic integration," *The Guardian* (January 31, 2002) at https://www.theguardian.com/theguardian/2002/jan/31/guardianweekly.guardianweekly1

though these two examples involve Muslim communities, these acts are not unique to Muslim communities—not even close (and most Muslims abhor these acts, incidentally). My point in using these examples is to illustrate the lengths to which some members of some communities will go, to the point of killing their own family members, to ensure that outsiders are never let into their communities, or to ensure that insiders never interact with outsiders. Racism is everywhere, and no type of color-coding (as in, "persons of color") should be allowed to mitigate or obfuscate the abject disgrace of this ugly act wherever and whenever it is perpetrated.

Why assimilation is not a dirty word
There is something else in play with all of these examples, including the two tragedies just described, that needs to be emphasized. This whole discussion began with a re-evaluation of claims about cultural relativism and the claims put forward by some groups that any expectation of assimilation by mainstream society, regardless of context, is an unreasonable and unacceptable request, one that presages cultural diminution of minority communities and hence undermines the practice of diversity. As I suggested at the start of the discussion, one of the ways out of the endlessly frustrating rhetorical morass of debates over cultural relativism is to shift the perspective slightly so that culture is not the main issue involved. This is not a sleight-of-hand trick; it is a justifiable tactic because culture is not usually the main issue involved—it gets invoked because it is usually the most convenient device to preclude the possibility of meaningful dialogue or debate (which ironically is one of the things cultural diversity is supposed to produce). More often than not, the debate is really about *situational ethics*, about discerning the right thing to do or not do in a complex environment where absolute values may not be readily discernible.

Consider the commonly occurring experience of a family relocating from one country (home country) to another (host country), with the added complication that the host country has a dominant culture that is markedly different from the home country. This scenario will work whether the relocation was involuntary (such as refugee flight) or voluntary (such as immigration for better economic opportunities). Although we are often taught to see this in terms of culture shock, or a learning moment in tolerance, there is also an ethical element to this that is far too often overlooked. If a family were to flee their country of origin due to fears over insecurity and relocate to a new country where they were able to find peace and security, there should be a moment of reflection—yes, even in traumatic circumstances—where that family tries to understand why their new environment has such peace and security to begin with. If the country whose safety they seek and want to enjoy has created this better environment due to the values and practices of the host country, is it ethically justifiable to take advantage of the safety produced by those values and yet simultaneously reject the influence of those values because they are "foreign"? The same question remains valid if the reason for the relocation is voluntary. Is it ethically justifiable to take advantage of better economic opportunities created by the values and practices of a host country, and yet simultaneously reject those values or minimize one's absorption of those values on the grounds that they are "foreign"? Again, this is not a question of cultural relativism, but rather a question of ethics. If the safety or refuge or the enhanced economic opportunities you enjoy are produced by a certain set of cultural values and practices, then ethics and respect require you to adopt those values as well. It is an ethical way of giving back to the host community whose benefits you enjoy.

Once again, from a different angle, we bump into our old friend, assimilation. And once again, we need to take a few steps back to determine whether this word really deserves its much-maligned reputation. The first thing that is necessary to point out is that assimilation comes in a variety of guises: it can be state-induced and coercive, or it can be a matter of individual choice. I agree with those who oppose state-led policies of coercive assimilation, but it's because I oppose the coercion, not the assimilation. You cannot force someone to adopt a set of beliefs; at best, you can only force them to act as if they have those beliefs, whether they actually hold them or not (and if you try to force them on someone they most likely will not). Coercive assimilation programs led by the institutions of the state are bound to fail and are more likely to generate a backlash that will make them counter-productive or more oppressive in the long run.

Assimilation *as a matter of individual choice*, however, is something altogether different. With individual choice, this is where the question of ethics becomes so important. I have suggested earlier in this book that diversity is something of a civic duty, a civil act of participating in society with a propensity for negotiating identity-based issues in the most constructive manner. Ethically, that means choosing the actions that best benefit both self and society; it is neither purely a selfish act, nor purely a selfless act. But any system of ethics worth its name would have to lead necessarily to the conclusion that anyone benefitting from a system or even wishing to benefit from a system of values and practices has an ethical obligation to enter that system and participate in that system by assimilating to its core principles. Anything else would amount to what ethicists and economists alike refer to pejoratively as "free-loaders"—those who never enter or participate in a system and yet enjoy the benefits that flow from it.

The second point that needs to be made here about assimilation is that it is not an all-or-nothing process; indeed, by any meaningful definition of diversity, it cannot be so. Diversity rarely has absolutes, and one of the challenges of cultivating and maintaining a vibrant system of social diversity is that much of it requires the dexterous negotiation of opaque and grey areas that have no easy answers and produce frequently uncertain outcomes. But if we know that absolute assimilation is not possible or even desirable (absolute assimilation would produce uniform sameness and hence would eliminate diversity), and if we know that no assimilation at all is absolutely unethical (no assimilation would be a society of free-loaders), then partial assimilation is the requisite goal of any society hoping to cultivate a vibrant and productive system of diversity. The question then is, how much assimilation is enough?

The short and simple answer is this: *as much as possible*. But as with all things related to diversity, nothing is ever as simple as it seems. In this case, the key variable in question is the realm of the "possible." How do we know how much assimilation is possible? It is actually easier in this case to approach the question from a negative direction and confront the claim often heard in discussions of diversity that non-dominant groups in the United States have tried to assimilate, but due to the exclusive racism of the dominant group, were forced to retreat to their own communities for protection and solidarity. There is considerable evidence in American history that for specific immigrant groups and in specific moments of time this had once been true as a matter of both policy and practice. I should say with absolute clarity that this undeniable fact will always remain a sad part of the American past. But those policies and practices are precisely that—a part of the American past—and as we speak, diversity as a policy and practice is a part of the American present. Whatever failed efforts occurred in the past, these should have no bearing on new efforts in the present. Diversity policies in the present are designed to integrate a diverse society together—this is, after all, the main premise of the *Grutter* decision—and so anyone who willfully accepts the benefits of those policies has an ethical obligation to participate in that integration, part of which means to assimilate to the values of American society. To assimilate, by the way, is not to surrender. It is to contribute. Assimilation does not destroy old values as much as create new ones. Everyone has the same ethical obligation to assimilate as much as possible, whether they come from a majority or minority position.

Keep in mind also that in relation to barriers that have excluded minority and immigrant groups into mainstream society, the United States is no different than any other country in the world. All societies struggle with exclusion and marginality. Indeed, if there is anything unique about the United States in this regard, it is the extent to which it goes out of its way to reverse the unfortunate legacies of the past and provide avenues of inclusion for every single different community in the country. I have been fortunate enough to live and work in several other countries, and it has always been a challenge and a struggle to find acceptance as an outsider and a newcomer in any society and any community I have encountered. It would have always have been the easier route to complain about the difficulties and just find other Americans already living in these areas and hang out with them (note interestingly how American who do this abroad are often called "ugly Americans"). But it would also be something of a failure and also, I think, highly unethical to do so. So instead, I have always done everything I could possibly do to find acceptance and gain the respect of my host community, wherever I have lived: learning the language, learning local customs and etiquette, learning pretty much everything it would take to be an integrated member of the community. It takes a lot of work, but I do it because it is the right and ethical thing to do. While it is a very slow and often frustrating process, with very few exceptions it has always worked well for me. It has *always* been worth the effort. Again, it would always be the easier route to find a pre-packaged community of Americans and bypass the whole process, but to do so would be to miss the whole point of what a diverse community should be and what diversity itself is supposed to do.

What I find particularly strange about the *enclave mentality* of so many identity groups in the United States, in which various communities justify community involution based on the putative difficulty of entering mainstream American life, is that many members of these communities are utterly intolerant of the reverse situation. I know many Korean-Americans, for instance, who spend most of their time in the Korean-American community and with Korean-American friends, working on Korean-American issues, and doing things that cultivate Korean culture. While much of the insularity is justified in terms of the difficulty of "breaking in" to American culture, it is more accurate to speak of the difficulty of "breaking out" of Korean-American cultural circles. What I find most interesting however is that if I mention Americans (or other non-Korean foreigners) I know who live in Korea and who face far greater challenges trying to enter Korean society, most ethnic Koreans will become indignant. The solution, they say, is for the Americans to assimilate as quickly as possible to all things Korean, to understand and appreciate Korean ways, and not to engage in "foreign" practices or to cling to any "foreign" values. Apparently, only assimilation can lead to acceptance in Korea, though the same Korean-Americans complain of not being fully accepted in America unless they assimilate. In America, it seems, they don't want to "lose culture."

This is not just some idle speculation, and I have in fact seen this in action first hand. During a summer in South Korea at Yonsei University in Seoul, one of my close friends and colleagues—from the United States and not ethnically Korean—was engaged in a conversation with another Korean person and confessed that he was not a big fan of Korean food. The Korean person with whom he was talking suddenly became agitated, and asked him bluntly and directly: "Then why are you here?" And this is not something that is limited to South Korea, either. I was once told by a faculty member in Singapore, just prior to my departure from California to go to Singapore for a sabbatical, that I should "not bring my American ways with me."

What these types of interactions collectively tell us is that there has been far too much emphasis on issues of cultural relativism and far too little emphasis on the *ethics of diversity*. Indeed, ethics rarely enters the debate at all, and so we are left with endless discussions of cultural difference that usually go nowhere and end up creating a lingering sentiment of mistrust and mutual suspicion—again, the very sorts of things that diversity is supposed to overcome. Assimilation has become something of a dirty word in the ongoing debate on diversity, and has become associated with the idea of a loss of culture, making assimilation a negative thing that is to be avoided at all costs. Diversity as cultural relativism ends up creating nothing more than *involuted enclaves of identity* where refusal to assimilate is lauded as a proud desire to preserve and celebrate one's own group-based identity. The question of whether that stance is ethical or not rarely enters the picture, and it seems to me that there is no way that diversity can achieve the goals of social justice and social harmony with which it is associated unless the ethical questions of diversity are moved to center stage. There is an inherent contradiction in taking the stance that a person can be simultaneously a part of (it is wrong to keep me out because I am different) and apart from (it is wrong to include me because I am different) American society, based upon self-professed group-based identities. This contradiction is produced by an ethical inconsistency: one cannot say "count me in" when the benefits of diversity are offered, but "count me out" when the responsibilities of diversity are expected. This is not a passive predicament created by what is presumed to be the victimization and marginalization of minority groups by the majority population; rather, it is a conundrum produced by a failure to choose and a failure to engage ethically with the actions required of all members of society in contributing towards a workable version of diversity. Diversity only works when everyone works together.

Committing to diversity
Aside from the oft-invoked excuse of cultural relativism in any of its many guises, there is another important line of reasoning that is similarly employed in order to put the brakes on the necessary actions required to create a vibrant and productive sense of diversity. This usually takes on the lexical moniker of something like "not forgetting one's roots." This is not to deny that people have roots—everyone has roots, of course—but we have a variety of roots, only some of which are truly and genuinely cultural. We are complex trees, all of us. So when a person or a group offers forth the claim that they cannot assimilate to mainstream society because to do so would dilute their culture and they want to preserve their culture, what I hear is not a plaintive cry to protect and preserve a culture on the verge of disappearance, but rather a diffident rationalization of what is in essence a fear-of-commitment issue. "Not forgetting one's roots" is a progressive expression that masks a conservative fear of change. Keep in mind also that trees have *individual* roots, not collective ones. So keeping true to your roots is to keep true to your own sense of self, not to your group identity.

I find it interesting and not a little amusing that individuals and groups that resist assimilation and integration using excuses such as the my-culture-values-family line of reasoning do not understand that diversity only works when society is viewed as a larger social family, and if there is one thing that family requires to hold together, it is commitment. Yes, diversity requires commitment. Just as one cannot say to their spouse, "I want this marriage to work out great but I also want to keep dating my ex on the side in case it doesn't," one cannot say to a society whose safety and security are provided by the integrative practices of diversity, "I want to enjoy all of the benefits that are provided by these groups who have committed to building this diverse society but I want to avoid assimilation and integration myself so I can protect and preserve my roots, in case things don't work out." Anything less than full commitment usually spells doom as much for marriage as it does for diversity.

So what exactly does full commitment look like? As I made clear earlier, full assimilation is not an acceptable or even desirable request, since full assimilation ends up producing a homogeneous society, nullifying the whole point of diversity. So full commitment to diversity is not synonymous with full assimilation. To use the marriage analogy one more time, it would certainly be accurate to state that while most people expect full commitment in a marriage, no one assumes that in a marriage each spouse should strive to become like the other. So full commitment must be something other than a simple request for assimilation. There are few things that are simple in the world of diversity, and so it is probably best to describe the characteristics of what full commitment would look like, rather than offering a simplistic step-by-step and one-size-fits-all formula of the sort that makes policy-makers and self-styled community activists drool with naïve delight.

First, full commitment is an individual act and an *individual choice*. There is no other way to break through the group-think that muddles and obfuscates the realization of diversity. The individual must commit fully to diversity.

Second, full commitment is an *active choice*, not a passive one. All too often, diversity activists and proponents assume that persons of color automatically contribute to diversity by virtue of their presence. Take a "white" office environment, and then add a few persons of color, and voila!—you have a diverse work environment. This is a very appealing interpretation of diversity to some since it requires no real effort, but it is sheer stupidity to think it will lead to anything useful. You are more likely to have created a work environment of different people, none of whom is truly committed to making diversity work, in which case you will have transformed an all-white dysfunctional environment into a diverse dysfunctional environment—hardly an improvement and hardly worth the effort. The same level of commitment is required of all members of a diverse society, regardless of their background and regardless of their position in society relative to everyone else.

Third, full commitment is a *leap of faith*; there are no guarantees of anything. Diversity itself is something of a leap of faith, and full commitment means dedicating oneself to the process of constructing a diversity that works, even if some of that process renders up a string of epic failures. Diversity is not something you commit to only as long as it pays back in direct, immediate, and tangible benefits. It is a long-term process, much like democracy, that gets better over time, but requires hard work, commitment, and continuous cultivation from everyone and anyone. The majority of people currently advocating for diversity in the United States are not really advocating diversity as a social good; they are advocating it as a form of social vengeance or a form of narcissistic community advancement. When diversity does not procure or provide either of those desired outcomes, more often than not, these people retreat back to their respective communities because supposedly diversity "failed them." This helps nothing and no one. Continuous retreat or loss of faith makes for a start-and-stop pathway to diversity, a sort of "one step up and two steps back" that leaves everyone frustrated, suspicious, and disillusioned. That's hardly a workable approach for diversity.

The reason that this strategy of continuous retreat is not a workable approach for diversity is that the end result of continuous retreat is an *enclave society*. Yes, there have been enclave societies for thousands of years and in a wide variety of different cultural contexts, but that does not make enclave societies practical or even desirable. There is a good reason for this, a reason that is missed or ignored by most historical commentators who like to write on how other societies were diverse in the past, and that reason is this: *Enclave societies are not diverse societies.* An enclave society is a cluster of non-diverse communities living contiguously but with minimal interaction. If you could take each enclave neighborhood and pick it up with a giant forklift and move each diverse neighborhood ten miles further away from all the others, the result would not be noticeably different. Enclave societies are a classic example of what I earlier described as *passive diversity*—the mere coexistence of different groups that turns out to be an illusory form of diversity, one that offers the appearance of diversity without the substance. Active diversity requires *interaction* and more importantly it requires *commitment to interaction* from the individual members of all of the communities. The idea of continuous retreat is therefore neither socially nor ethically justifiable, largely because it creates a situation in which at least some of the groups in society expect and demand substantive benefits *from* diversity while engaging in actions that undermine and in fact preclude substantive contributions *to* diversity.

Culture and exile
One of the things that makes diversity such a challenge, continuously so, is that there are very few if any areas where anything is certain or where the rules are truly black-or-white. For instance, another grey area in the world of diversity is the role and contribution of what might be termed *exile communities.* America currently plays host and has historically played host to a number of exile communities, that is, communities that seek refuge and respite in the security of American society due to traumatic events and experiences in their home countries that make living there untenable and impossible. Exile communities differ from immigrant communities due to their different time horizon and different array of

expectations: immigrant communities come to start a permanent life in a new country, whereas exile communities come to seek temporary refuge with the hope of returning to their home country as soon as it is safe or possible to do so. Most exile communities choose to seek refuge in societies that are safe and stable—that is, when and if they have the possibility to choose—which means they are often benefitting from the social dynamics of the society whose protection they enjoy. One example of this would be the large Burmese community in the San Francisco Bay Area, most of whom fled from the brutality of decades of military rule in Burma, particularly since 1990, when Burma's brief moment of democracy was crushed (though there has been a tentative return of democracy in Burma since 2010). In the case of the Burmese community in the San Francisco Bay Area, as with all other similar cases of communities living in exile, host societies cannot and should not expect the same type of commitment, because with the intent to return to their original homeland, exile communities have a vested interested in preserving much of their cultural patterns and practices, to make the return from exile as efficient and as effective as possible. In the case of temporary exile, full commitment to assimilation may not be a constructive option for the community.

The more difficult question comes when exile communities transition wholly or partly into immigrant communities. This can happen for a number of reasons, ranging from a growing realization that the situation that created the need to seek refuge is not going to resolve in the home country to the growing sense of comfort in the host country that can lead to a change of heart and a desire to settle permanently in the host country. But whatever the reason, the question emerges of whether the exemption to participate fully in the construction of diversity in the host society still remains. The answer, it seems clear to me, is that it does not. Once the decision is made to settle permanently in a country, then whatever the original intent may have been for arriving in the country, the ethical obligations transform and the commitment to join society and participate fully in diversity begin. Once the transition occurs, the exemption disappears. One of the major problems with diversity in America is that too many groups and too many individuals from those groups are looking for exemptions from their commitment to diversity and the responsibilities it entails. American diversity has far too many communities looking for ways out, when what we need are all communities looking for ways in.

The unembedded individual
In the winter of 1995, I had an opportunity to live in London for a research project in which I was engaged that required me to access the impressive archives at the British Museum. As a result of personal and professional connections I had made at the time, I ended up staying with a South Asian (I don't want to identify here which specific part of South Asia) family in the borough of Hounslow, in the southwestern part of Greater London. The South Asian family with whom I stayed were living in London because they had fled the fighting and violence of their home country. They had fled to the security and safety of Great Britain, and had managed to build a reasonably prosperous life in London that would not have been possible in the corrosive and hate-filled environment of their homeland at that time.

One of the first things I noticed was how deeply embedded they were in a relatively small circle of family and friends who all came from the same part of South Asia. Not surprisingly, this kind of deep cultural embeddedness produced the same type of judgmental attitudes and myopic arrogance often associated with any type of cultural narcissism. I was told rather shortly after my arrival, for instance, that I should avoid any of the stores owned and operated by Gujarati people, because Gujaratis were "cheats" and couldn't be trusted. In case any reader is tempted at this point to reach for the universally useless justification that such attitudes were imbibed as a result of centuries of British colonialism in South Asia, save your breath. This was a stereotype that had nothing to do with British imperialism or racism but was instead embraced by these persons only after arriving in the UK. I know this because I was told by them that their attitudes were developed through the alleged experience of being cheated one too many times by various Gujarati merchants, who were apparently, according to what I was told, just a deceitful group of people—all of them (as I have said, racism is truly and disturbingly diverse). And it wasn't just the restricted social circles that surprised me; there was also the fact that this family, like so many others I met in Hounslow, had never gone out to participate in the tremendous diversity that London had to offer.

I discovered, for instance, that this family had never gone out even to try a different kind of cuisine at one of the thousands of different sorts of restaurants that London has to offer. I decided therefore to do something special and nice for them, or at least what I thought might be special and nice, and cook an Italian dinner for them in their home, so they would not have to venture out to a "foreign" restaurant and could enjoy something new and different in their own home. I made them a simple but classic Italian pasta dish—linguine with a mushroom cream sauce—using the best Italian ingredients I could find, something that was easy to do given the availability of pretty much everything in London. When I served the dinner, however, the reaction was not what I was expecting. There was silence for a few minutes, until finally one of the members of the family spoke up and said: "Really, this is what they eat? It's just bland and tasteless." (Incidentally, I'm not a chef, but I do know how to cook.) At that point, she went to the kitchen and brought back a jar of chili sauce and dumped it all over the pasta. Once she had masked and destroyed all of the "Italianness" of the dish, she then proceeded to eat it with delight. In other words, once the moment of diversity was neutralized and everything was rendered uniformly and homogeneously South Asian, only then were things once again acceptable.

This whole episode illustrates one of the central challenges of making diversity work in any environment or context, and that is the challenge of inducing individuals to leave the comfort zone of their own homogeneous culture and to enter the "foreign" worlds of others. Without that, diversity can never succeed. While there have been many proponents of diversity—and usually not a week goes by at UC Berkeley without some event articulating this viewpoint—who think that the task of diversity is to make dominant groups ("whites" in the American context) feel uncomfortable as they are forced to admit their privileged and oppressive ways and make adjustments and sacrifices accordingly to stop their incessant oppression, the reality is that this approach to diversity is a one-sided and misinformed act of historical vengeance that has never worked and never will. Among the many realities of crafting a new diversity: *Diversity will make everyone equally uncomfortable, at least in the short term.*

The reason that diversity will make everyone uncomfortable, at least in the short term and in the transitional stages, is that all persons, and not just some, will need to *unembed* themselves from the comfort of their own group and venture out into the uncharted, intercultural territory that exists when we are out among others. This isn't just a reasonable expectation in order for diversity to work. It is a necessary one. And the goal of leaving one's homogeneous comfort zone is not to make everyone "lose" their culture, but rather to make the diversity of society itself an inclusive comfort zone. Diversity should not be the place we enter occasionally when we want to see things that are bizarre and different, after which we return "home" to our respective groups. And diversity should not be something we are force-fed through soporific "sensitivity training" seminars that kill both brains cells and sensitivity with equal alacrity. It should be a place where all sorts of different individuals come together and feel equally at home. The key word here is *individuals*: diversity is an act of different individuals, not a collection of different groups.

Making culture foreign
Once again, we are back to the question of the individual and the role of individualism in the larger framework of diversity. To reiterate what was clarified earlier, individualism is not something that is synonymous with selfishness or even self-interest—even Western ideologies and cultures frown on pure hedonism—but rather about developing well-informed preferences at the individual level. We have already seen the damaged and distorted choices that are made when group-think and involution are in motion, so it stands to reason that only when the individual steps out of any environment where group-think or involution is in motion can she or he develop a set of well-informed preferences. Unexpectedly, then, it is only when individuals leave the group or groups of which they are a part that they can freely choose diversity as a preference, and it is only with the free choice of diversity as a preference that the individual commitment that is so essential for the success of diversity can happen. Diversity is therefore fundamentally an act of *individual agency*.

It is important to point out that leaving the group to develop one's individual preferences is not the same thing as abandoning the group, nor is it a permanent or irrevocable act. I am not suggesting in any way that all members of society should renounce any and every link they have to the social groups that played some role in their social and personal evolution. But the requirements of diversity do create the obligation to render all groups equally foreign, if only for a moment, so that our new choices and preferences reflect our awareness that other options are available and of equal validity. In essence, even if we choose to stay within our original group, we do so as a form of re-choosing that group, as an act of

Understanding the Misunderstanding

making a well-informed choice about the qualities of that group rather than as a languid act of identity-based pride.

In one of the lesser-known works of the extravagantly creative Japanese writer Haruki Murakami, interestingly titled *Underground* in both the English and the Japanese versions, he reflects upon the social forces in Japanese society that led to the terrorist attack (using sarin gas) on the Tokyo subway in 1995 by the religious cult Aum Shinrikyo. Murakami makes the unsettling observation that the excessive conformity of Japanese society has had the unfortunate side-effect of pushing all forms of individual expression and personal creativity deep underground, where they fester and suppurate until they reemerge as paroxysms of violence against the society that put them there in the first place. This observation, which in essence takes one of the key elements that gives most members of Japanese society a sense of comfort—the element of identity-based homogeneity—and turns it into a discomfiting social affliction, is already interesting enough. What is even more interesting in the context of our current discussion is that Murakami had been able to develop this perspective and reach this conclusion only because he was able to step outside of Japanese society—at the time of the Tokyo subway attacks he was a resident scholar and writer at Princeton University—and reexamine Japanese society as an outsider, in this case with the help of a new, American perspective. It is the type of valuable insight that diversity can provide, but only if we first take the revolutionary step of leaving the comfort of our groups to develop new perspectives drawn from the many different ways of seeing the world. This is precisely what I mean by the *unembedding* of the self.

One of the benefits that diversity is supposed to produce is the gradual reduction if not elimination of cross-cultural and intergroup misunderstanding, the most extreme form of which (and the most well-known) would be racism. We could include in this any other similar form of derogatory stereotyping as well. And yet, as anyone not living underground can easily see, so far this has not happened. So far down the road of diversity we have supposedly come, and yet there is still racism and stereotyping everywhere one looks. Quite frankly, about the only thing that current practices and policies of diversity have produced is an unfortunate strain of putrid resentment. The question we continuously return to is why—why hasn't diversity created a sense of social harmony and social justice? The central problem we still have is that our current practices and policies of diversity seem unable to dislodge the profound misunderstanding and mistrust that exists between different groups, and the reason for this is that we are still trying to create a passive platform of diversity that consists of the mere coexistence of different groups. "This is what diversity looks like!" proclaimed the cast of *Orange is the New Black* on stage at the Screen Actors Guild awards in 2016. They were referring to the fact that many individuals in the cast represented different minority groups in American society, and there they were, assembled side by side on the stage to display diversity. The problem with that claim—and this is not meant to disparage the show in any way—is that diversity doesn't have an *appearance*. It has a *substance*. Putting people on a stage like so many different dolls in a display case doesn't do anything for anyone, and it doesn't do anything for diversity. If we are confusing appearance with substance, it is little wonder that diversity hasn't lived up to its promise.

The misunderstanding and mistrust that are still so prevalent in American society—and again, the misunderstanding and mistrust move in all directions with equal vigor, and not just from dominant groups toward non-dominant groups (the oppression hypothesis)—emerge from a lack of circulation of ourselves among others. This is why a diversity based on the mere coexistence of different groups, the display on the stage approach, or what I call *passive diversity*, will always fail. *Active diversity* requires the individuals of each different group to walk away from their group and circulate equally among others, to walk *among* them and to walk *with* them and to walk in *their* shoes and to talk in *their* language. This is the type of true commitment, of individual commitment, that it takes to create a diversity that works effectively and works equally well for everyone. We can and should learn simultaneously *from* others and *for* ourselves.

The alphabet soup of diversity
Among the South Asian community in the United States, there is a term that is sometimes used, sometimes overused, to describe second-generation South Asians (children born in America of immigrant parents): ABCD. It is an acronym that stands for American Born Confused Desi.[27] The last term requires a bit of explanation for those unfamiliar with the South Asian community. It is a term that refers to someone from South Asia: des (pronounced *desh*) means country and desi (pronounced *deshi*) means someone who is from the country, which in this case refers mostly but not necessarily exclusively to India. The whole idea behind being an ABCD is itself a confused mess but it does speak to many of the problems that continuously and consistently undermine the project of diversity. The "Confused" part of the ABCD epithet is supposed to refer to the fact that such persons are torn between different aspects of their identity, mostly due to the difficulty of fitting in within American society. An ABCD is American-Born, but Confused because he or she is different from what an American is supposed to be, and that difference stems from being a Desi.

The term is inherently antithetical to the idea of diversity on multiple levels. First of all, if a person is American-Born then

---

27 For an amusing take, see Anita Mehrotra, "28 Ways You Are Absolutely An American Born Confused Desi Girl," *BuzzFeed* (March 31, 2015) at https://www.buzzfeed.com/anitamehrotra/28-ways-you-are-absolutely-undeniably-an-abcd-girl?utm_term=.buaZyy1wgv#.bbYRPPmoMw

they can't also be Desi. From a different angle, we again bump up against something we discussed earlier: on the one hand the word Desi gets used by Americans of South Asian descent, referring to both American-born and South-Asian born persons, and on the other, there is the complaint that mainstream American society has a racism problem because it often cannot differentiate between American-born and South Asian-born persons. The ABCD problem seems to be a self-inflicted problem, an implicit claim that anyone outside of mainstream American society ("white society") is confused because they have no place to belong, foreign in America due to Desi values but foreign in the Des because of American values. Then again, if you call yourself Desi, you already have one foot outside of America at all times, so it might not be mainstream society that is at fault here.

I also find the idea that anyone in America who is not white and mainstream is automatically in some sort of identity crisis a bit disingenuous. One of the fundamental weaknesses of the current state of diversity in America is that it encourages everyone to think of their own confusion as somehow the product of an identity-based incongruity that was forced upon them in some inherently oppressive process. There is this persistent belief that the "white folks" of mainstream American society are well-adjusted and happy, and that their biggest moment of anxiety, if ever they have one, is deciding which shade of white paint to choose when they paint their picket fences. But subscribing to this view of diversity in America is a bit like someone with a fear of public speaking hiring Keith Richards as an eloquence tutor: in the end, you are really only trading one problem for another. Identity-crises and every other sort of identity-based dysphoria occur with all people, regardless of race or gender or ethnicity or religion. A Muslim in America might be having a crisis of faith not because of America's allegedly imperialist agenda or because Native Americans were oppressed by Columbus, but rather because he or she is having a crisis of faith in their own personal world for very personal reasons. If our sense of diversity cannot tell the difference between the two, then our sense of diversity is senseless.

The fact of the matter is, for every person who thinks they are an ABCD and that this is somehow a by-product of the inherent oppression of America's demographic inequality, there is another South Asian in America who is struggling to find his or her own pathway in spite of the conformist oppression of his or her own "desi" culture. I once had a student of Indian heritage who was absolutely in love with Shakespeare and wanted to major in Shakespearean studies. His parents were mortified and were threatening to stop paying for school. Aside from the fact that his parents thought that only stupid people studied anything other than science (science was for smart people, literature was for dumb people), there was the additional issue that Shakespeare wrote in English, the language of the colonizer, and so according to his parents it was an unsuitable topic for a South Asian to study. Never mind that the language of instruction at UC Berkeley is English—with that, his parents apparently had no issue. He was certainly American Born and Confused, but it was his Desi parents who had Confused him more than anything.

My absolute favorite retort to the whole set of acronyms that exist to describe various elements of marginality and oppression that supposedly pervade American society comes from a wonderful person I met who was originally from Cambodia. She described herself as an AABC: American Accidentally Born in Cambodia. Growing up in Cambodia as a woman, the restrictions on individual creativity, especially on women, and the cultural pressures to conform to a narrow spectrum of life choices, restricted her opportunities to cultivate the thoughts, dreams, and imaginings that she had. In America, however, she found a true kindred spirit, a place to let loose and explore each of those opportunities, to become the person she dreamed of being in Cambodia, but could only be in America.

In a way, being "AABC" is exactly what the American dream is: the dream to be something different and the freedom to pursue that dream as far as possible. The American dream is not a pizza that you should expect to be delivered in thirty minutes or else you get your money back. It is rather a feast of the imagination that may take a lifetime of effort and commitment and in the end may or may not be realized or achieved. What the American Dream offers is the chance to reinvent and reconstruct our lives, a sort of recurring dream that allows us to keep trying over and over again in the hopes that at some point we will finally get it right. There is no guarantee that we will get it right, but we can at least keep trying.

Finding a place for culture
The role that culture plays in the process of self-invention and in American society in general is often lost in discussions of diversity, and when it is not lost, it is otherwise manipulated, distorted, and perverted to serve ends that are not justified by their means. America does have a culture, and it is the culture of individual choice. Yes, we all know that no person is an island, but no person is a group either. It is hypocritical to make the individual choice to come to America, only to resist becoming a part of American society on the grounds that individual choice is not valued in one's culture. To invoke the idea of diversity to argue that a plurality of cultures should be allowed to coexist, each on their own terms, is to willfully neglect the idea at the heart of diversity that the goal is to integrate a diverse amalgamation of identities, not to diversify American society into separate enclaves. This is what makes diversity, and along with it democracy, the long-term and arduous

projects that they are. To join one's own cultural group and to embrace the pre-fabricated set of values that this cultural group putatively professes, usually by suppressing diversity within the group, is to short-circuit that hard work and to short-circuit the process of diversity. *It is anti-diversity masquerading as diversity.* It is a form of civic torpor in which groups invoke the desire to opt out of American society to protect their own cultural values, without realizing that opting out of American society to form a separate cultural enclave induces a self-fulfilling process of weakening American society from within. One cannot cite the absence of a coherent culture in America as a reason to opt out if opting out is precisely what precludes the formation of that coherent culture. Diversity should *break* this cycle of illogical and circular reasoning, not entrench it, and certainly not reward it.

Incidentally, if one were at this point wondering why it is a negative thing to assimilate to the values of one's specific identity group but a positive thing to assimilate to American society at large, it goes back to the suggestion—a necessary ingredient for diversity to work—that diversity must be an active process, rather than a passive one. Simply belonging to a group and assimilating to those group values, for instance, is a thoughtless and passive process. If a Latino wants to be in a Latino group, then membership is automatic by virtue of existence. But to assimilate to American society, with its myriad of different groups and identities—this is a process that requires active negotiation and active interaction with things that are foreign to the ways of our otherwise passive group existence. This is why diversity is about situating ourselves among others, and this is why diversity is something we must all do together. If we retreat to our separate enclaves and groups, we have what is in essence a grassroots system of self-inflicted apartheid, rather than anything that remotely resembles an integrated, diverse society.

Making diversity move
There have been a number of metaphors that have been employed in different moments of American history to try to describe the demographic and multicultural composition of American society. At one point America was known as the melting pot, but in more recent years, as various opponents and activists have championed the idea that refusal to melt—as in, to integrate or assimilate—is somehow a heroic act of resistance, we now have different descriptive terms. America is a mosaic, for example, because it shows a coherent image and yet each tile remains separate. Or America is a salad bowl, because even when America's salad gets tossed, each of the different items in the salad—tomatoes, croutons, lettuce, and so forth—remain visibly separate, though they contribute to the overall taste of the salad as a whole. No doubt there will be more such culinary metaphors to emerge in the future, but it seems to me that it is not to the pantry we should be turning to find a descriptive term for what makes America what it is.

Instead, we can look to other forces found in nature. Earlier I pointed out the pitfalls of cultural *involution*, in which identity-based groups turn inward and gradually create distance between themselves and other groups in society. It would stand to reason that if cultural involution creates deleterious effects for diversity in America (and for diversity anywhere), then something that is the opposite of that, or near to the opposite of that, would at least represent a more salutary version of how a diverse society should function. It seems to me that the opposite of cultural involution would be cultural *convection*. Convection is a complex concept that shows up in the worlds of geomorphology, where it refers to the continuous transfer of heat from the core of the earth to the surface (thus producing the pressures that generate plate tectonics), and oceanography, where it refers to the churning of oceans created by the interplay of hot and cold currents and the transfer of heat from the equator to the poles. For those who insist that diversity in American society must be described by some food-related item, I can at least offer a reminder that there is such a thing as a convection oven, which heats food more efficiently by using fans to distribute the heat evenly and by facilitating the circulation of heat throughout the oven, thus preventing the formation of isolated hot spots—heat enclaves, if you will.

In relation to diversity and multicultural societies, *cultural convection* refers to the continuous interaction and intermixing of groups and individuals to generate new social patterns, new social currents so to speak, that continuously inaugurate alternative possibilities for the recalibration of social relations. As much of a mouthful as that seems—I am aware that it veers dangerously close to the sort of bombastic drivel that academics famously belch forth—it at least makes clear how its antipodean counterpart, namely cultural involution, works its corrosive magic on whatever promise or whatever potential diversity has. Cultural convection is perhaps a fancier way of expressing one of my central points throughout this book, which as a reminder is this: for diversity to work, it must be *intercultural*, not multicultural. When identity-based groups opt out of society, even partially, on the grounds of preserving their culture, and when individuals recuse themselves of their commitment to diversity, for whatever reason, the currents of convection begin to atrophy, creating in essence a persistent version of a social El Niño. Out of that, one can expect nothing more than a string of diversity-related disasters.

The role of culture is not irrelevant in relation to diversity, but at the same time, it is not and cannot be the center of gravity. Diversity requires all participants to shed their cultural baggage, perhaps not entirely but at least to the extent where the unencumbered and unembedded individual is allowed to venture forth into the intercultural spaces of society, both to influence the social currents produced by the cultural convection of diversity as well as be influenced by them. Any recipe for diversity that allows individuals to remain comfortably embedded in their cultural environments is promoting either an enclave society, which is not diversity anyway, or else is a form of diversity too heavily burdened by free-loaders to succeed. In a time when so much sensitivity toward identity politics is creating a truncated dialog that restrains free expression, the reality is that culture—that vague phenomenon that seems to evanesce any time we try to pin it down with any sort of precise meaning—has to be put in its proper place in order for ourselves to move freely and meaningfully among others. Rethinking the centrality of culture in our lives is simultaneously the most discomfiting and most liberating thing we can do, and yet without doing it, without letting go of our most cherished ideas about who we are and where we come from, even for a moment, diversity simply cannot ever sing the beautiful song it was destined to sing. If we are lucky, we will hear at best only the plaintive swan song of diversity, or more likely, we will be left with the unbearable shrill of cacophonous noise. If diversity is to be orchestrated properly, we must all learn to play our instrument well, which means that for diversity to work, for diversity to play its sweet-toned tune, it is going to take practice. Lots and lots of practice.

INDEX

A
ABCD (American Born Confused Desi), 187
affirmative action
    in practice, 138
American Dream (as myth), 74
assimilation
    necessity of, 169

C
caste system
    in India, 134
China
    and Western ideas, 159
    refugees, 93
classroom
    exchange of ideas, 50
Confucius, 160
Convection
    cultural, 192-193
critical mass
    as diversity, 26-28
cultural relativism, 157

D
diversity
    active vs. passive, 9, 12-14
    as inherent good, 26-29
    intercultural, 11
    public and private, 140

E
education, 33
embeddedness
    as problem, 181
English language, 64-65
ethics
    and diversity, 169-170
exile communities, 179

F
family
    and culture, 162-163
Filipinos
    as Asian, 78
foreign language
    study of, 124-126

G
Goethe, 22
group-think
    opposite of diversity, 141-143
Grutter v. Bollinger, 26
Guess Who's Coming to Dinner, 166

H
hate-speech
    diversity of, 102-103
hyphen-of-convenience, 133

I
immigration, 64
involution
    as anti-diversity, 117-118

M
Mississippi Masala, 79-80
multiculturalism, 11
Murakami, Haruki, 185

O
oppression, 154-155

P
perpetual foreigner, 77
PETA, 43-45
potato chip
    theory of, 146-148
Proposition 209, 115
Pussy Riot, 157

R
racism
    diversity of, 6-8
refugees, 91-96
roots
    and identity, 176

S
safe spaces, 53
Sahindal, Fadime, 168
Sichuan peppercorns, 129
Smith, Adam, 144-145
South Korea
    minorities in, 132-133
student groups
    identity-based, 122
study abroad
    and diversity, 126-128

V
voting blocs
    identity-based, 154

ABOUT THE AUTHOR

D. C. Zook is a writer, musician, and filmmaker who also happens to be a professor at the University of California, Berkeley, in the departments of Global Studies and Political Science. He writes both fiction and nonfiction, and cultivates both sense and nonsense. He is currently at work on two books, one on new frontiers of human rights and the other on the changing landscape of cybersecurity. He is also plotting his next novel, and plotting many other things as well.

Visit D. C. Zook at dczook.com

www.ingramcontent.com/pod-product-compliance
Lightning Source LLC
Chambersburg PA
CBHW071731080526
44588CB00013B/1986